Weird and Wacky
WASHINGTON PLACES

Bree Coven Brown & Lisa Wojna

**BLUE
BIKE
BOOKS**

The Publisher: Blue Bike Books
Website: www.bluebikebooks.com

Library and Archives Canada Cataloguing in Publication

Brown, Bree Coven, 1972–
    Weird and wacky Washington places / Bree Coven Brown and Lisa Wojna.

ISBN 13: 978-1-897278-47-5
ISBN 10: 1-897278-47-0

    1. Washington (State)—Miscellanea. I. Wojna, Lisa, 1962– II. Title.

F891.B76 2008   C813'.6   C2008-901419-7

Project Director: Nicholle Carrière
Project Editor: Kathy van Denderen
Projduction: Jodene Draven
Cover Image: Courtesy of JupiterImages
Illustrations: Roger Garcia, Patrick Hénaff, Graham Johnson, Peter Tyler

We acknowledge the support of the Alberta Foundation for the Arts for our publishing program.

PC: P5

CONTENTS

ACKNOWLEDGMENTS

Eternal thanks to my husband, Garrett Michael Brown, for keeping me well fed and well loved, and for seeing me through many long nights at work on this project. I am indebted to generous friends who readily shared their favorite Washington places: Faye Hoerauf, resident Wenatchee expert; Marcie Wirtz, researcher extraordinaire; Katy Beaudreau, Andrea Luke, Darcie Syme, Ross Aker and Cindy Riskin; and to Jess Thomson and "Oyster Bill" Whitbeck for sharing their oyster expertise. I am especially grateful to the Seattle Public Library's Greenwood branch. Love always to my Dad and Nancy, to my wonderful in-laws and to my dear friend Lea Policoff for supporting me in everything I do. And special thanks to editor Kathy van Denderen and publisher Nicholle Carrière for the wonderful opportunity to explore my weird and wacky side.

–Bree

Many thanks to our clever editor, who pieced together the work of two authors and did so seamlessly, to my co-author, Bree, and to my family—my husband Garry, sons Peter, Matthew and Nathan, daughter Melissa and granddaughter Jada. Without you, all this and anything else I do in my life would be meaningless.

–Lisa

INTRODUCTION

Lots of places claim to be the center of the universe. But Fremont in Seattle actually has the sign to prove it! Before you pooh-pooh the plucky assertion, take stock: does your hometown have a Solstice Parade where naked bicyclists zoom past a Volkswagen-eating troll and a statue of Vladimir Lenin on their way to a working Korean-made rocket inscribed with the motto "Freedom to be peculiar"...in Latin? Didn't think so!

Fremont is just one example of the eccentric Evergreen State, where Bigfoot is an officially government-protected species and locals worship at the Church of God-Zillah (in Zillah, Washington). People are so law-abiding here that jaywalking is regarded as a heinous crime, yet legendary D.B. Cooper—the skyjacker who jumped from a Boeing 727 over the Cascade Mountains in 1971 with $200,000 in ransom money and was never seen again—is honored with "D.B. Cooper Month" every November, and Washingtonians re-enact the Last Great Horseback Robbery in Oakville each July. While the next big empire is hatched at Starbucks headquarters, and the latest technology is produced at Microsoft campus in Redmond, traditions are steadfastly maintained in Poulsbo, where the annual Viking Fest celebrates the town's Norwegian heritage. Gourmet restaurants crowd big cities like Seattle, while Conconully, population 200, hosts the Testicle Festival and Cowboy Caviar Fete in homage to the prairie cowboy delicacy of bull testicles.

What follows is an irreverent love letter to all that makes Washington weird and wacky. This book could just as easily (and accurately) be called Cool and Fascinating Places. Buckle your seat belt and get ready to witness fascinating freaks of nature like the mysterious Mima Mounds, a flaming geyser in Auburn and Jake the Alligator Man. Explore artifacts such as the Olympic Peninsula's "Pompeii in the Mud" and one of North America's oldest known human remains of the Kennewick Man.

We'll pay our respects at the graves of Bruce and Brandon Lee, and take a trip up 79 flights to one of America's Best Bathrooms (yes, they give awards for that kind of thing). Indulge your sense of the macabre with a literary drive by the Ted Bundy's University of Washington dorm room (where he supposedly kept some of his victims' heads). Vicariously visit memorials to Dirty Biter the Dog, and Jimi Hendrix, each loved by many in their own way. Hear spine-tingling accounts of Tacoma's Old City Hall, where the bell towers ring when no one is there. Decide for yourself whether the Native American ghost dances at Glenacres Golf Course because it was once ancient burial grounds.

Washington is full of weird, wacky and wonderful surprises—such as the Bettie Page house, a private home with a 17-foot-tall mural of pin-up icon Bettie Page painted on its side. The painting is fully visible off the I-5 highway—and next to a Mormon Church—but it still inspires more compliments than complaints.

This book is chock-full of enough fun facts and phenomena to make the most skeptical reader agree—even if it weren't already home to the first UFO sighting, the Space Needle, and the world's first Science Fiction Museum—that Washington State is out of this world.

Freaks of Nature

Washington is known for its natural beauty. Residents awake to say, "The Mountain's out," referring to majestic Mount Rainier (kept close company by the equally awe-inspiring Olympic Mountains). Western Washington has the Pacific Ocean, Puget Sound and Lake Washington; the east has rolling hills, fertile farmland and wine country.

And all that rain (which is less than you'd think) is what makes everything lush and green and gives us our nick-name, the Evergreen State. Then, every once in a while, Mother Nature throws us a curveball to make our pictur-esque life more interesting. From the catastrophic to the bizarre, we'll cover the unusual terrain of Washington's strangest naturally occurring phenomena, lovingly referred to as freaks of nature.

NATURALLY OCCURRING PHENOMENA

MIMA MOUNDS
LITTLEROCK

Washington's greatest geological mystery has puzzled scientists and residents alike for more than 150 years. Mima Prairie, a Puget Sound lowland in Thurston Country, is mottled with 4000 odd lumps, each between 5 and 7 feet tall and up to 40 feet in diameter. The mounds stretch across 450 acres. No one really knows what caused the bizarre formations: were they shaped by earthquakes? Glaciers? Gophers? Could they be alien-created inverted crop circles?

Northwest explorer Captain Charles Wilkes is credited with discovering the mysterious mounds in 1842. He thought they might be Native American burial mounds, but there were no bones inside, only stones. Many scientific papers have suggested explanations, but their only uniform agreement is that the mounds are indeed surreal. Surprisingly, gophers are currently the leading theory behind the mounds' formation. Professors Paul Dalhquist and Victor Scheffer from the University of Washington cite the northwestern Mazama pocket gopher as the likely source of the pimpled plains. Pocket gophers are small, but they tunnel away from their nests and could theoretically displace a large amount of soil over time. And you thought the gopher holes in your garden were bad!

Development has destroyed many of the mounds, which once numbered more than one million, but the Nature Conservancy, National Park Service, and nearby Evergreen State College in Olympia rescued the rest. Mima Mounds is now a Natural Area

Preserve. Similar formations as far away as China, Africa and South America are all called Mima Mounds in honor of Washington's Mima Prairie, the original, quintessential mound phenomenon.

GINKGO PETRIFIED FOREST
VANTAGE

Ginkgo is called the "living fossil" because the same species of tree has endured since dinosaurs roamed the earth—literally. Ginkgo ancestors date back 270 million years and can be found in Eastern China, but wild specimens are virtually extinct in North America. That's why it's so exciting to catch this rarity among an entire petrified forest right here in Washington.

The Ginkgo Petrified Forest State Park preserves the fossilized remains of what was once a lush forest overlooking the Columbia River. Lava buried 50 species of trees (including redwood and sassafras) in a basalt tomb, where silica slowly replaced the wood and hardened it into stone. The rarest variety of petrified wood, ginkgo, was discovered by highway workers in the 1930s, which led to the declaration of the 470-acre state park as a historic preserve and, later, a national natural landmark. Is it any wonder Washington state's gemstone is petrified wood?

POMPEII IN THE MUD
OZETTE

Five hundred years ago, as people were going about their daily routine of cooking, whaling and building canoes, the entire Makah Native American village on the Olympic Peninsula was suddenly submerged in a mudslide and buried alive. The remains were preserved in detail, earning the site the nickname "Pompeii of North America." Artifacts discovered by hikers in the 1970s led to an archaeological dig that unearthed an unprecedented view of ancient Makah life, the most comprehensive picture ever found. Whole families were frozen in action in complete Cedar longhouses with intact hearths. More than 50,000 artifacts were excavated, including fishing gear, canoes, woven baskets, primitive tools, stored food, entombed dogs, even whale remains. The collection is on display at the Makah Cultural and Research Center at Neah Bay.

APE CAVE
VANCOUVER

There are no apes in Ape Cave: it's named for the sponsor of the brave Boy Scout Troop that first explored it in-depth—the St. Helens Apes. At an amazing length of 12,810 feet, Ape Cave is the longest lava tube in the continental U.S. It rests on the western slope of Mount St. Helens. The lava tube was formed almost 2000 years ago when flowing lava cooled so quickly it solidified around the molten middle. When the inner lava eventually drained away, the outer crust of lava remained. Basalt flows such as the one that formed this tube are rare in the Pacific Northwest—they're more typically found in climates like Hawaii.

Ape Cave is now an official National Volcanic Monument, part of the Gifford Pinchot National Forest, and is open to the public. More than 100,000 visitors per year go 20 feet beneath the earth's surface to explore the cave, dropping from ladders that lead to the main entrance. Would-be spelunkers take note: the upper cave is 1.5 miles long, averages about 42° F and descends into complete and utter darkness. The United States Department of Agriculture Forest Service instructs visitors to bring no less than three sources of light when they visit the cave. In some sections, the cave's roof yields to natural skylights. In other spots, the roof is 30 feet thick. Highlights of the Ape Cave–dwelling experience include the 70-foot-wide Big Room, 8-foot lava fall and a lava ball erupting from the ceiling. Don't touch the walls, though; they're coated with mucousy, light brown cave slime, a life form that dies upon contact (and probably feels pretty gross).

KENNEWICK MAN
KENNEWICK

When two young college students snuck in to watch the hydroplane races in July 1996, they didn't expect to come across a 9000-year-old human skull in the Columbia River or to indirectly spark a legal controversy about the man's origins. The partially buried human remains, dubbed the "Kennewick Man" for the eastern Washington city where they were found, led to the discovery of one of the oldest and most complete human skeletons unearthed in North America.

Forensic anthropologist James Chatters, who helped police recover the skeleton, noted an unusual observation: the Kennewick Man's skull structure appeared to be "Caucasoid";

in other words, European or white, not Native American, as remains of that age were previously presumed to be. This discovery complicated assumptions about when exactly European settlers immigrated to the Western world. The find also ignited public debate in a tug-of-war between scientists, who wanted to study the skeleton, and local Native American tribes (the Umatilla, Yakama, Nez Perce, Wanapum and Colville) who wanted to give the man a proper burial.

Because the Kennewick Man was found on federal property controlled by the U.S. Army Corps of Engineers, his remains technically belonged to the government. The Feds were prepared to hand the skeleton over to the tribes—until a group of eight scholars sued for the right to pursue scientific inquiry. The coveted bones were locked for safekeeping in the Burke Museum at the University of Washington, where they remain to this day. In August 2002, the court ruled in the scientists' favor, allowing continuing study of the Kennewick Man and his mysterious ancestry.

FLAMING GEYSER
AUBURN

The Flaming Geyser once spewed fire and gushed water several feet high in a fantastic display that earned it a place in "Ripley's Believe It or Not." The geyser is now past its prime, with a moderate seep of methane gas lit to create a flicker no more than 6 to 10 inches high. But locals still carry a torch for this flame—after all, how often do natural gas emissions spark right out of the ground? The flaming geysers are actually methane seeps that were caused by a hole drilled into coal beneath the earth's surface in 1911. This mining test hole also resulted in the smaller Bubbling Geyser, which emits a stream of mineral bubbles. Once privately owned (before the owners let it go bankrupt in the 1960s), the area is now Flaming Geyser State Park.

DRY FALLS
COULEE CITY

Dry Falls is more than an oxymoron; it's practically the eighth wonder of the world. Dry Falls is all that remains of the largest waterfall that ever existed. Carved out by Ice Age floods from Glacial Lake Missoula, the falls' dramatic cliffs plunge 400 feet where water once rushed 3.5 miles wide, shaking the earth in the process. Compare that to Niagara Falls' paltry drop of 165 feet and width of a mere mile—in its glory days, Dry Falls was more than 10 times the size of Niagara. Today it's a deep, dry gorge, part of the Grand Coulee Canyon and the sprawling 4027-acre Sun Lakes-Dry Falls State Park.

SOAP LAKE
GRANT COUNTRY

When a lake leaves frothy piles about one foot high, and passing winds stir up sudsy white foam, what else can you name it but Soap Lake? The water in this lake is permanently stratified,

which means its layers haven't mixed for thousands of years. The result? A filmy texture that easily floats, just like a bar of—you guessed it—soap.

This eastern Washington lake has been studied by NASA and the National Science Foundation. It seems the water at the lake's bottom is five times saltier than ocean water and contains 17 natural minerals, from sulfate and potassium to titanium and tungsten. Soap Lake has been heralded for its medicinal properties and is dubbed "Miracle Lake." In the 1920s, people flocked to the area to bathe in and drink the water, which was rumored to cure Buerger's disease, a form of gangrene that afflicted many veterans of World War I. The afflicted reported that a Soap Lake bath a day kept amputation at bay, and noticeably improved their condition. Some local hotels still pipe Soap Lake water into their rooms, and the town water fountain offers Soap Lake water from one of its two spouts.

The healing powers of Soap Lake have yet to be proven, but the water does contain ichthyol, an oily substance distilled from a mineral containing fish fossils. (The ichthyol in Soap Lake probably comes from decomposing brine shrimp.) Ichthyol is sold over the counter in Europe to treat acne, eczema, skin abscesses and psoriasis.

With the advent of modern medicine, however, the town of Soap Lake has shriveled to a quarter of its former size and glory, but people still come here to get away from it all. And they still drink the water (even though it's quite pungent).

THE DUNGENESS SPIT
SEQUIM

The Dungeness Spit is the longest natural spit in the United States, and one of the longest in the entire world. What's a spit, you ask, besides a tool for roasting pork over a fire? It's a narrow strip of land, in this case sand, that juts out into the sea. The Dungeness Spit is 5.5 miles long—and growing about 15 feet per year as the wind and surf transport sand and gravel to the area. Most Puget Sound spits straighten out a ragged shoreline, or stretch in a thin, direct line out into a body of water. The Dungeness Spit protrudes from the Olympic Peninsula like a large arm with unusual hooks and jags, right into the Strait of Juan de Fuca.

The strait is a hectic shipping channel for the ports of Puget Sound and British Columbia, but the sand spit is a haven. Literally. Most of Dungeness Spit is protected as the Dungeness National Wildlife Refuge. More than 250 species of birds have been recorded at the spit, including the black brant, described by an educational display as "A Goose with Problems." The slightly better-adjusted harbor seals and Orca whales also live in the refuge, accompanied by 41 species of land mammals. Dungeness crabs, a staple of the popular Pacific Northwest fish stew cioppino, scurry about south of the spit, in shallow Dungeness Bay. Ten thousand birds winter in the refuge, and birdwatchers flock to see them. A short trail winds through the forest to a view of the spit in all its glory and leads down to the beach where the real treat awaits. The historic and beloved Dungeness Lighthouse sits at the tip of the spit and is well worth the 4.5-mile beach walk to see it up close.

Established in 1857, the lighthouse is one of the oldest in the Northwest. The Coast Guard used to run it, but when they decided to close it down, the New Dungeness Light Station

Association offered to take it over rather than lose access to the area. Since 1994, the lighthouse has been staffed around the clock by volunteers who cheerfully lead tours of the light tower up 74 steps. The Dungeness Lighthouse also provides unique accommodations for die-hard nature-lovers: you and your family can stay inside the lighthouse for a week if you're willing to give tours, mow the lawn and serve as an official lighthouse keeper. However, the opportunity is limited to association members, who pay up to $315 per adult for the privilege. But it's hardly a well-kept secret. This working vacation currently has a two-year waiting list.

WASHINGTON ROCKS

Washington rocks. And not just because Nirvana and Pearl Jam started here. Washington's rocks rock. They make up some of the state's most fascinating and bizarre landscapes.

LINCOLN ROCK
ENTIAT

Before there was Mount Rushmore, there was Lincoln Rock. So how come no one's ever heard of it? Back in 1889, Billy Schaft took a photograph of a prominent basalt rock outcropping in central Washington. His friend Ed Ferguson noticed that the rock bore an uncanny resemblance to Abraham Lincoln's profile. The men pronounced it Lincoln Rock and entered the picture in a photography contest put on by *Ladies' Home Journal*. To their surprise, it won first prize and was published in the magazine and circulated nationwide. The publicity generated enough interest that the name "Lincoln Rock" became official. Lincoln Rock State Park, acquired by the state in 1980, rests on the east side of Lake Entiat, where President Lincoln's famed silhouette is still visible across the water.

THE DEER HEAD
MOUNT RAINIER

Another rock of ages, the Deer Head has endured for, well, ages on Mowich Face, the northwest face of Mount Rainier. "Mowich" is the Chinook tribe's name for "deer." The Mowich Face (and Mowich River below) was so named because Native Americans saw the face of the Mowich in the mountain itself. Just below the summit, on the northwest side of the peak, jutting rock, clefts and snow form a large deer's head, neck and antlers. The buck's nose turns downward and to the right. The Deer Head is visible from as far away as Puget Sound, depending on the amount of snow on the mountain. Legend has it that the Deer Head brings good luck to those who can find it. Back in 1911, John H. Williams, in his book *The Mountain That Was God*, wrote "the deer of rock is there still." And so the deer remains today, as do those who search for its head.

MOUNT ST. HELENS
SKAMANIA COUNTY

In 1980, my mother picked me up from school in a T-shirt decorated with burn holes that read "I survived Mount St. Helens," immediately destroying any chance I had at popularity. Mount St. Helens is no laughing matter to Washington or the families of the 57 people it killed. Among the casualties was 83-year-old Harry Truman, a mountain resident for more than 50 years who famously refused to heed evacuation warnings. "If the mountain goes, I'm going with it," said Harry. His lodge was buried under 150 feet of volcanic debris, and his body was never found.

Those who survived the eruption on the morning of May 18, 1980, faced enormous loss. The explosion demolished 250 homes, 47 bridges, 150 square miles of timber and 185 miles of highway. The economic toll reached $1 billion. It cost the local government more than $50 million just to clean up the ash,

which blanketed 6000 miles of roads. Visible ash extended to 11 states, and the mountain itself lost more than 1000 feet off its top, leaving a mile-wide crater in its wake. The Mount St. Helens National Volcanic Monument was created to preserve the volcano and its aftermath for future study.

The nearest town, Castle Rock, nestled between the Cowlitz River and I-5, capitalizes on the tourism wrought by the disaster. A Castle Rock brochure trumpets the town's claim to fame as "The Gateway to Mount St. Helens." For years, Mount St. Helens erupted every 45 minutes on the giant screen of the local Cinedome movie theater. Thrill-seekers could "Experience the Eruption" from stadium seats that rumbled along with the explosions. The Academy Award–nominated film's appeal eventually fell dormant like the volcano itself, and sadly, the Cinedome shut down in 2007.

Mount St. Helens came alive again on March 8, 2005, sending billows of ash and steam nearly 6 miles into the air. The only active volcano in the continental United States, Mount St. Helens has actually been in continuous, gradual eruption since the fall of 2004. She rumbles still, but the drama is contained to the film...at least for now.

BIG
GARGANTUAN &
RIDICULOUSLY
OVERSIZED

BEACON ROCK
Skamania

Rock on! Beacon Rock is the second largest rock in the world, trumped only by the Rock of Gibraltar on the Spanish peninsula. This free-standing monolith towers 848 feet high, presiding over the great gorge of the Columbia River. The modest road marker at milepost 35 reads "remarkable high detached rock," which does not begin to do it justice. Beacon Rock is an enormous, stand-alone, single block of stone representing the core of a nine-million-year-old volcano lost to river erosion. The peak, reachable by a three-quarter mile trail (if you can endure the 52 switchbacks) yields a breathtaking panoramic view that encompasses the Columbia River Gorge, Oregon state's Mount Hood and Washington's Mount Adams.

Beacon Rock was so named by Lewis and Clark on their expedition to the Pacific Ocean on October 31, 1805. In their journal, they recorded the rock as a landmark. Six years later, the John Jacob Astor expedition set upon the same structure, which they decided to call Inoshoack Castle. It was known as Castle Rock for more than 100 years, until the United States Board of Geographic Names officially restored the original Lewis and Clark moniker in 1916. Native Americans continue to refer to Beacon Rock with their own name, *Che-che-op-tin*, which means "navel of the world." Thirty-five miles east of Vancouver, Washington, near the Oregon border, Beacon Rock is now a 4650-acre state park.

Out of this World

The world's first UFO sighting was reported in
Washington in 1947. The state has the nation's second-
highest number of UFO sightings and is home to the
National UFO Reporting Center. Presidential candidate
and U.S. congressman Dennis Kucinich claims he had
a UFO encounter outside Shirley MacLaine's house in
Graham. The world's first science fiction museum debuted
in Seattle, as has a paranormal museum and a space
travel supply company for all your otherworldly adven-
tures. Science fiction writer and founder of the Church of
Scientology, L. Ron Hubbard, spent his formative years in
Bremerton. The moral of the story? You don't have to go
to the top of the Space Needle to know that Washington
State is out of this world.

UFOS, THE SPACE NEEDLE AND SCI FI, OH MY!

THE WORLD'S FIRST FLYING SAUCER

MOUNT RAINIER

Is it something in the water? Ever since the world's first UFO sighting was reported near Mount Rainier in 1947, Washington has been abuzz with claims of strange objects hovering above the state. The National UFO Reporting Center in Davenport, Washington, which describes itself as being "dedicated to the collection and dissemination of objective UFO data," has logged 2642 UFO reports to date, more than any other state in the country except California. As recently as November 2007, the reporting center website documented calls about "a large saucer" hovering above LaConner for an hour, a bright green fireball flashing for a few seconds in Shoreline and a mysterious orange light shining steadily over Tacoma.

Washington is the epicenter of UFO history, which began on June 24, 1947, when pilot Kenneth Arnold was flying from Chehalis to Yakima, searching for a missing military plane. Amid crystal-clear skies, he saw a formation of nine boomerang-shaped aircraft moving erratically between Mount Rainier and Mount Adams, "like a saucer skipping across water" (hence the term "flying saucers," coined by a reporter, not by Arnold himself). He calculated that they were moving at about 1200 miles per hour, a supersonic speed three times that of any manned aircraft of the era. A U.S. Air Force investigation did not contest that Arnold saw what he saw—their report stated, "It is the present opinion of the interviewer that Mr. Arnold actually saw what he stated he saw. It is difficult to believe that a man of [his] character and apparent integrity would state that he saw objects and write up a report to the extent that he did if he did not see them." Yet the Air Force officially declared Arnold's sighting a "mirage." By then, the public had already caught on. In the following weeks, hundreds of similar reports of "flying saucers" flooded in. On July 4, 1947, Frank Ryman of the U.S. Coast Guard took the first photograph of a UFO from outside his home in north Seattle. Kenneth Arnold died in Bellevue, Washington, in 1984, but the flying saucer craze he started lives on.

Some folks, especially locals, believe Arnold's sighting was actually predated a few days by the so-called "Maury Island incident." Maury is a small island in Puget Sound near Tacoma. On June 21, 1947, harbor patrolman Harold Dahl was out on his boat when he apparently saw six large, doughnut-shaped aircraft hovering 2000 feet above the water. Dahl even said that a flying saucer fragment fell from the sky, injuring his son and killing his dog, which they buried at sea. Dahl collected UFO debris as "evidence" to show military intelligence officers, who dismissed the whole affair as a hoax. But the next day, the same two intelligence officers, Captain Davidson and First Lieutenant Frank Brown, were killed in the Air Force's first plane crash over Kelso, Washington. UFO enthusiasts believe that despite the officers' disregard for Dahl's report, the plane was carrying the evidence as classified material. Some even claim to have found black slag rock at the crash site 60 years later.

Misfortune continued following the crash. The more Dahl talked about what he saw, the worse his luck became. His business failed, his wife became ill and his son disappeared and resurfaced states away with amnesia. Dahl finally recanted the story after what he described as an intimidating visit from a "Man in Black" at a Tacoma café. Dahl's experience was the first-ever documented case of a visit from Men in Black (MIB), preceding UFO research pioneer Al Bender's famous 1953 MIB visit. The meeting with the mysterious MIB silenced Dahl. Following the encounter, all he would say was that the Maury Island UFO incident was a hoax. But the legend lives on at the Seattle Museum of the Mysteries, whose owners display what they call newly discovered remains recovered from the crash in Kelso. Decide for yourself with a visit to the bizarre museum.

SEATTLE MUSEUM OF THE MYSTERIES
SEATTLE

Washington's "only paranormal science museum," the Seattle Museum of the Mysteries, is operated by the Seattle UFO/ Paranormal Group in Seattle's Capitol Hill neighborhood. The museum's exhibit of Kenneth Arnold features a tape recording of Arnold's first interview about what he saw, a rare first issue of *FATE Magazine* from 1948 with his first-hand account, and an original copy of his book, *The Coming of the Saucers*, published in 1952. Even more intriguing is the museum's Maury Island exhibit, which displays surface debris from the Air Force's first plane crash that "could be an artifact" from the Harold Dahl UFO sighting. Museum directors Philip Lipson and Charlette LeFevre recovered the curious item in 2007 in a wooded area in Kelso owned by James Greear, where the plane crashed 60 years earlier. They continue to investigate the mystery.

The Seattle Museum of the Mysteries covers more than just UFOs, though. The modest, library-like space—with walls lined with the type of books that appeal to conspiracy theory fans—documents all kinds of Northwest legends and lore. There's a section on Bigfoot (of course) that includes four footprint casts, and a furry Bigfoot statue that all but screams "photo op," as well as some Uncategorizable Fun Oddities, such as photographs of Washington crop circles from Chehalis and Eltopia, a wax head of D.B. Cooper, and Seattle's only oxygen bar ($5 for a five-minute treatment). The museum also runs ghost tours and features a haunted "lock-in" with its own ghost, mad scientist Nikola Testa.

MEL'S HOLE
ELLENSBURG

The Seattle Museum of the Mysteries gives periodic lectures on Mel's Hole in Ellensburg, but it seems to be the only museum that still believes in it. A guy named Mel Waters rose to local fame in 1997 when he called in to Art Bell's Coast to Coast AM radio show (KOMO AM in Seattle) claiming there was a paranormal pit on his property that was at least 15 miles deep and could resurrect the dead. Well, animals, at least. Mel said his neighbor disposed of a dead dog in the hole but then saw the dog alive and well, romping in the woods days later. Ten million rapt listeners tuned in. Mel said the bottomless pit was used as a neighborhood dump for old refrigerators and dead cattle, but somehow it never filled up. He tried to measure the hole himself by inserting a fishing line into it, but he gave up at 80,000 feet.

Even before Mel's claims, locals in Ellensburg had traded tales of a hole so deep no one could see the bottom. Children threw rocks down it, but the stones made no sound. Ellensburg also has had more than its fair share of UFO sightings, and the paranormal community searched for Mel's Hole for years. They never found it. Then the *Tri City Herald* newspaper reported that there was no Mel Waters listed on the tax roll or in the phone book; in fact, there was no evidence that he even existed outside the radio waves. Even when questioned, Mel would not surrender contact information, subscribing to a frustrating "don't call us, we'll call you" philosophy. In his last call to the show in 2002, Mel claimed he sold the property with the hole on it, and he won't tell anyone where it is. Art Bell and the radio network refused subsequent interviews, claiming it was all a hoax. Nonetheless, a few diehards still make pilgrimages to Ellensburg, but most believe Mel's Hole was a *hole* lotta something about nothing.

SCIENCE FICTION MUSEUM AND HALL OF FAME
SEATTLE

Truth may be stranger than fiction, but science fiction is strangest of all. Just ask Paul Allen, billionaire co-founder of Microsoft, who founded the world's first Science Fiction Museum and Hall of Fame in Seattle in 2004. The museum was off to a good start with $20 million of Allen's own collectibles. Located in the same building as the psychedelic Frank Gehry–designed Experience Music Project, the Science Fiction Museum is marked by a glowing alien spacecraft above the entrance. It hosts Science Fiction Film Festivals as well as opportunities to meet notable authors of the genre and view originals of their work, but the costumes are the main attraction at the museum. Lots and lots of costumes. On display are Batman's signature mask; Darth Vader's helmet; Captain Kirk's shirt; Terminator 2's metal face; a *Star Trek* Klingon warrior suit; a *Battlestar Galactica* cylon costume;

Buck Rogers' XZ-38 disintegrator pistol, circa 1938; the pointy hat worn by the Wicked Witch of the West; and the actual Alien Queen from the movie *Aliens*.

The museum is a geek's dream come true in a city where geekdom is celebrated. (I'm including mysef in this assessment. Geek pride!) The pop-culture icons on display are complemented by a comprehensive timeline of science fiction literature, NASA-issued spacesuit gloves and the (in)famous telecast dupe "War of the Worlds," by Orson Welles, which convinced the general public of a make-believe Martian invasion. And did I mention E.T. lives here? You can go visit him and tell him in person to phone home.

GREENWOOD SPACE TRAVEL SUPPLY COMPANY
SEATTLE

Meanwhile, in North Seattle, the Greenwood Space Travel Supply Company offers close encounters of a unique kind. Signage for the "interstellar emporium" exclaims, "Space travel is all we do," but that's not exactly true. Behind the (literal) curtain of this chrome space-age storefront lies 826 Seattle, a non-profit, free writing center for children, founded by author Dave Eggers, best known for *A Heartbreaking Work of Staggering Genius*.

The space travel theme is a clever mode to lure inquisitive youngsters into the building, where all purchases of ray guns, Dark Matter brand rocket fuel, astronaut ice cream and gravity-in-a-can benefit the free writing center, which also offers after-school drop-in tutoring at no cost. It's like a theme party for a cause. It doesn't take a rocket scientist to figure out that to get children to want to learn, you have to appeal to their imagination. And in this case, it works: about 35 children show up every day to get help with their homework or to take part in creative

writing workshops. The youngsters also contribute to the museum itself. The Youth Advisory Board, staffed by high school students, decided to give one of the poles in the building a name: Bill. Because it's their space, it was their decision, and now Greenwood boasts the only Space Travel Supply Company, and writing lab, with a pole named Bill. The organization also offers fundraising Mustache-a-Thons for the grown-ups, in which men grow mustaches over a five-week period and get supporters to sponsor their hair growth.

THE ROBOT HUT
ELK

Tucked away on a farm in Spokane County is a big red barn. No surprise there. They're as common in rural America as grazing cows and horses. But in this particular barn near Elk, there's another must-see, private collection—and this one you've really got to see to believe.

It seems John Riggs, owner of the 2000-square-foot barn, took a keen interest in robots. Yes, robots. And while we might all think they're pretty cool, and have maybe even purchased an R2D2 figure once upon a time, it's hard to imagine just how many kinds of robots are out there. John has a considerable portion of those varieties. In fact, he has more than 2500 in his one-of-a-kind collection, and he moved to the country and built the barn specifically for the purpose of showcasing them and sharing them with others. Touring his museum is like walking into a veritable warehouse of C3P0s, robocops, terminators, time machines and every other robot movie replica you can think of in just about any size you can imagine. Then, of course, there's the section set aside for John's own creations and re-creations, such as the Robo-Rigg with Nike "Eat My Dust Buster Shoes" and the B9 robot from *Lost in Space*.

METEORITES
WATERVILLE AND WITHROW

It's a bird! It's a plane! It's a...meteorite? In 1917, central Washington got a different kind of rain: a meteor shower. Several large meteorites landed in Waterville, weighing more than 100 pounds collectively. The largest, at 82 pounds of solid nickel and iron, became known as *the* Waterville Meteorite after a farmer ran over it and broke his grain harvesting machine. Farmer Fred Fachnie loaned it to the Washington State History Museum in Tacoma, which tried to claim the space rock for its own. The Waterville sheriff got it back, though, and it's now on display at the Douglas County Historical Museum, alongside another meteorite found in nearby Withrow in 1950. This celestial rock had a contrasting composition and was from an entirely different meteor shower. (What is it with celestial phenomena and Douglas County?) If solid extraterrestrial bodies don't do it for you, the museum also has a two-headed calf.

AND, OF COURSE, THE SPACE NEEDLE
SEATTLE

No book about Washington would be complete without a tip of the hat to our most recognizable symbol—the Space Needle. The signature structure was built in less than a year by John Graham for the 1962 Seattle World's Fair, which had a futuristic Century 21 theme, hence the flying-saucer-shaped top. (Among the colors used to paint the Needle were "Astronaut White," "Galaxy Gold" and "Orbital Olive.") At the time, it was the tallest building in the West at 605 feet. The architectural wonder draws 20,000 people to it daily—enough to populate a small city. For such a scrawny-looking thing, it's managed to hold its own against 200-mile-per-hour winds and earthquake tremors measuring 6.8 on the Richter scale. The glass-fronted elevators are none too friendly for those with a fear of heights; they scale the full 520 feet up to the observation deck in a mere 40 seconds. The rotating deck and restaurant offer a dizzying view of the sparkling Seattle skyline, the mountains and Puget Sound. On a clear day you can see forever.

BIG
GARGANTUAN & RIDICULOUSLY OVERSIZED

IT'S A...PLANE?
Mukilteo

Dillon Works Inc. in Mukilteo takes the top prize when it comes to innovative ways of advertising its specialty business. According to the company's website, it can "design and [fabricate] almost anything"—and they seem to take a lot of pride in creating things that are a little out of the ordinary. Take the 26-foot-long, two-ton paper airplane replica perched over the company's entryway. Created in 1999 and made out of fiberglass, steel and wood convincingly blended to look like a yellow paper airplane, the giant eye catcher is labeled by some sources as the world's largest paper airplane.

Bigfoot

In metropolitan King County, Washington, Sasquatch
(a.k.a. Bigfoot) is a protected species. Farther south in
Skamania County, it is a crime punishable by law to shoot
or slay Bigfoot. All this legal protection for a creature few
have even seen...or have they? The state has the world's
largest Sasquatch organization and is a leader in scientific
research of the phenomenon. No wonder Bigfoot Central,
the name of the website run by locals from Bothell, boasts
that "Washington State is Bigfoot Country." Whether
you're a Bigfoot hunter, a true believer or just someone
who appreciates the kitsch factor of a giant hairy man-ape
lurking in the woods, there's no denying Bigfoot is a big
part of Pacific Northwest life and legend. And law.

BIPEDUS GIGANTICUS

SASQUATCH SIGHTINGS
SKAMANIA COUNTY, MOUNT RAINIER AND SKOOKUM MEADOWS

Bigfoot may or may not exist, but he permeates all aspects of modern life in Washington. The Sasquatch Music Festival draws headliners such as Coldplay and Bjork to the Gorge Amphitheater every summer. BigFoot Java's drive-thru coffee franchise dots the highways with 20 locations. Children in Spokane attend Bigfoot Preschool. Even our NBA basketball team, the Seattle Sonics, has a furry mascot named Squatch. For such an elusive creature, Bigfoot is everywhere. But who—and what—is he?

Legends dating back to the 1800s describe an enormous, hairy biped inhabiting the woods of the Pacific Northwest. Native American tribal stories go back even further (the name "Sasquatch" is a Native American word meaning "wild man"). Sasquatch-type creatures have been reported in many areas, predominantly in Washington, Oregon, and the Canadian province of British Columbia, but not all Bigfoots are created equal. Each region lends its own specific characteristics, forming its own version of the hairy giant.

Washington's Sasquatch has been described as 7 to 8 feet tall and weighing between 300 and 500 pounds. He is broad and barrel-chested, and he walks upright like a human. His face is part man, part ape, with a prominent brow ridge and little to no forehead. His head is disproportionately small and he has no discernable neck. Brown, black or red fur covers his entire body except his face, hands and the soles of his enormous feet. Bigfoot's footprints are usually around 16 inches long and 7 inches wide. Alleged photographs of those footprints are responsible for the name "Bigfoot." The shaggy-haired beast was originally called Sasquatch; "Bigfoot" didn't really catch on until 1958, when a logger named Jerry Crew discovered footprints in California. A photograph of Crew with a cast of the giant footprint was circulated nationwide by the *Associated Press,* and "Bigfoot" as we now know him was born. "Sasquatch" and "Bigfoot" are used interchangeably, with "Bigfoot" most commonly used in this region.

The majority of reports describe Bigfoot as a shy, gentle, nocturnal creature who prefers solitude (despite a supermarket tabloid's report of one woman who stated that Bigfoot fathered her child during a single encounter at Mount Rainier). Some believe he is an undiscovered species of primate. The late Grover Krantz, a professor of physical anthropology at Washington State University and expert Bigfoot researcher and author, argued that Bigfoot is a descendent of Gigantopithecus blacki, a giant ape that supposedly went extinct more than 200,000 years ago.

A faction considers Bigfoot to be a human relative. And, of course, there are many skeptics who believe Bigfoot and his supposed sightings are nothing more than folklore.

The existence of Bigfoot has yet to be scientifically proven. Much of the purported body of evidence to date, however, was collected here in Washington. Some of the clearest photos of what appears to be Bigfoot were taken in 1995 near Wild Creek below Mount Rainier. The well-known Skookum body cast was gathered in Skookum Meadows in the Gifford Pinchot National Forest, by Mount St. Helens, in 2000. "Skookum" is actually the local Native American Chinook tribe's name for the area's Sasquatch. The Skookum cast went beyond mere footprints to capture a muddy print of Bigfoot's entire left lower body (including hair!). Several leading U.S. specialists in primate anatomy concur that this impression is indeed a Sasquatch.

Collected evidence includes eye-witness accounts, photographs, tracks, film, hair, excrement, footprint casts, the half-body cast—everything *but* irrefutable concrete proof that Bigfoot is real. But that doesn't stop Washingtonians from believing in him.

Sasquatch was officially recognized by the Army Corps of Engineers in 1975 when he was included in the Washington Environmental Atlas as a species native to the state. The Skamania County Ordinance offering Bigfoot legal protection begins by stating, "there is evidence to indicate the possible existence in Skamania County of a nocturnal primate mammal variously described as an ape-like creature or a sub-species of Homo Sapiens." Olympia's Washington State Capital Museum packs in the crowds for a Sasquatch exhibition organized by the Washington State Historical Society. And scientific expeditions led by the Bigfoot Field Researchers Organization (BFRO) are scheduled monthly across the country and often sell out in advance.

Farmer Jim Baum was prohibited from selling his dairy farm in 1996 because apparently 13 of his 17 acres were designated as wetlands, home not just to Jim but to 350 species of endangered plants and animals. On the list of these inhabitants, squeezed in between the bobcats and the beavers, was "Bipedus Giganticus," Bigfoot himself. Baum has never seen a Bigfoot, on his land or anywhere else, but King County refuses to remove the shaggy-haired giant from the list of animals protected by the Sensitive Areas Ordinance.

If Bigfoot is just a fable, we're reluctant to give him up. Washingtonians cling to their Bigfoot theories the way children cling to Santa Claus. Perhaps Nietzsche has a theory about those who believe in Bigfoot, those who don't believe in Bigfoot and those who understand the need to believe in Bigfoot. Until someone uncovers satisfying proof that Bigfoot does or does not exist, his place is secure as Washington's most popular unsolved mystery.

If you're looking for Bigfoot, Skamania County in Washington is the place to go. The highest concentration of sightings (51 of the 422 recorded by the BFRO) has occurred here. It is also the place where "Sasquatch, Yeti, Bigfoot and Giant Hairy Ape are declared to be endangered species." Which, I suppose, is why the county created a Sasquatch Refuge. Skamania County ranked as number three of the 20 best places to catch a glimpse of Bigfoot in acclaimed researcher Loren Coleman's book *Bigfoot! The True Story of Apes in America*. Skamania County is also hunting country, so maybe Bigfoot does need that protection after all.

BIGFOOT'S FRIENDS

Not content with only Bigfoot, Washingtonians have developed many theories about the company he keeps in the forest…and of his distant air and water relatives from beyond.

CADDY
PUGET SOUND AND LAKE WASHINGTON

Every state seems to have a Loch Ness Monster of some sort. Why should Washington be an exception? Cadborosaurus, a.k.a. Caddy, is a long sea serpent named for his favorite hangout, Cadboro Bay, near Victoria, British Columbia. But Caddy is an international traveler, seen from Vancouver, BC, to Alaska and Oregon, including stops in Washington waters. According to reported sightings, Caddy was a frequent visitor to Puget Sound in the 1990s and apparently surfaced in Lake Washington as far back as 1965.

Descriptions of Caddy vary. Most often, he's described as 15 to 25 feet long, but some folks insist he's nearly 40 feet. He reportedly has an elongated neck and a small head that looks like it belongs on either a horse or a snake, depending on who you ask.

Because he spends most of his time swimming around British Columbia, Caddy is probably Canadian, but somehow, when traveling between Canada and U.S. waters, he never gets stopped at the border like the rest of us do. Good thing, since I doubt he has a passport.

MEN WITH WINGS
WESTERN WASHINGTON

Human beings usually fly inside airplanes these days, but Washington residents claim to have seen a different kind of flying man at least three times in the last 60 years. The first report came in 1948, when two workers in Longview both saw "three men in flying suits flying through the air" in circles, 250 feet up. The birdmen were next spotted in Chehalis, supposedly wearing goggles and carrying what looked like guns. This time, they flew close enough to reveal some sort of flying contraption strapped to their chests; in other words, the wings were not part of their bodies. All was quiet on the western winged-man front until the mid-1990s, when a lone birdman purportedly stood in front of a teenager's car near Lake Kapowsin before flying off. This creature was 9 feet tall and hairy with bird-like feet. He sounds less like a mysterious flying man and more like a Batsquatch. What's a Batsquatch, you ask? I thought you'd never ask...

BATSQUATCH
MOUNT RAINIER

Is Batsquatch a Sasquatch with wings? Although some describe glimpses of a flying Bigfoot near Mount Rainier, Batsquatch is generally thought to be a more colorful creature. Blue or purple, to be exact. A large, blue, winged creature was reportedly spotted at Mount Rainier in April 1994. His leathery wings and bloodshot eyes gave him the nickname "Batsquatch," because he resembled an enormous bat. A similar creature was spotted in the shadow of Mount St. Helens, but over there he's purple, with a head that's part ape and part bat. This pterodactyl-like primate is thought to be nocturnal and carnivorous; in fact, Batsquatch has been blamed for the mysterious disappearance of livestock, from chickens and goats to pigs and even cows, though no evidence exists of his crime, or even his existence. Open-minded researchers are divided between classifying this unknown species as a new kind of fruit bat or a North American winged monkey. Whichever it is, Batsquatch has his own fan club, and website, which displays comical "photographic evidence" and offers this little-known fact about the crimson-eyed creature: his "official" theme song, at least according to the fan club, is "Stayin' Alive."

GEODUCK
PUGET SOUND

Our last bizarre creature is definitely real. But you have to see it to believe it. The geoduck (pronounced "goo-ey"—rhymes with phooey—duck), or more officially the *Panopea abrupta*, is the largest burrowing clam in the world. A geoduck weighs an average of 2 pounds, but it can sometimes grow to be 6 feet in length and weigh up to 15 pounds. But that's not what makes it so distinctive. We'll be honest with you: the geoduck is somewhat obscene. The giant saltwater clam has a decidedly phallic neck, 6 to 8 inches long, that hangs out of its shell to one side. It's yellowish and flaccid and, well, vulgar. Live ones even squirt fluid in the sand. The geoduck is basically the fish market equivalent of pornography. It's actually illegal in Washington to possess a geoduck neck unattached from its shell.

Not surprisingly, some say the unusual mollusk is an aphrodisiac. Geoducks become sexually active around six years of age and keep at it well into their hundreds. They live to be about 145. Perhaps it's thought that by ingesting them, one will gain some of their virility. The "elephant trunk clam," as it's sometimes called, is also considered a delicacy. Geoducks burrow up

to 350 feet beneath Puget Sound and are the region's most profitable shellfish. You won't find them at the A & P (I don't even think we have A & Ps in Washington) or your corner supermarket; they tend to be found at specialty fish markets, especially in Seattle, and in Asian grocery stores.

The taste of a geoduck has been compared to abalone. I ate geoduck sushi once, in what I'll refer to as a hazing ritual when I was still new to Seattle. It was…chewy. I can't say I enjoyed it, but I feel braver for having done it. And it did make me feel a little "dirty."

Evergreen State College of Olympia has adopted the geoduck as its mascot. All their sports teams are named the Evergreen Geoducks. Even the school's motto, *Omnia extares*, is Latin for "let it all hang out," a tongue-in-cheek reference to Puget Sound's sexpot of the sea.

THE BURIED A-FRAME
Kid Valley

When Washington experienced one of the worst volcanic eruptions in North American history in 1980, ash and mudflows from an angry Mount St. Helens caused considerable damage. Some even say the eruption killed Bigfoot, and then there are those who believe he's alive and well, at least in a permanent, concrete sort of way. Standing watch near the Buried A-Frame, a local souvenir shop that survived the eruption but now operates a few feet underground, is a 28-foot-tall concrete statue of the big guy, making it a perfectly weird spot to snap a roll of film!

You Collect *What?*

Generally speaking, museums are pretty popular places. When you visit a new place, you usually want to learn a little something about the community, its past, its people and the like, and the best place to do that is at a museum. But if you dig around a little, you may uncover a gem of a place that goes beyond the typical displays and dusty archives and into a world of the weird and wonderful. A place where shrunken heads, eight-legged animals and dinosaur dung are the norm—not that excrement is all that exciting, but hey, when was the last time you saw dinosaur dung?

So, if you're toodling through Washington and looking for something to do, by all means check out the community-run museums—they've got a lot to offer. Just don't forget to also keep your eyes peeled for those out-of-the-way gems or the weirdness staring you right in the face.

WACKY MUSEUMS

THE WASHINGTON
BANANA MUSEUM
AUBURN

Ann Mitchell Lowell is bananas about bananas. Her Auburn home doubles as the Washington Banana Museum, the only banana museum in the Northwest. Ann is a librarian by profession and curates a collection of more than 4000 banana-related artifacts she's amassed over the last 30 or so years. Banana songs blast a welcome as you open the door to a handmade banana rug at your feet, along with an almost overwhelming sea of yellow. "Anna Banana," as her parents called her in a sign of things to come, has vintage banana ads and posters, banana peel smoking paraphernalia, antique banana cookbooks, a 1969 Chiquita banana ride-on toy, a banana lamp, banana cookie jars, banana jewelry, banana hot sauce, glow-in-the-dark banana boxer shorts, a refrigerator covered in banana magnets, and a banana Christmas tree, just for starters. Her pride and joy is a fiberglass Chiquita banana cello—that works! A walking encyclopedia of banana trivia, Ann will fill you in on the banana's history and remind you that it is the best-selling fruit in the United States.

Her collection started by accident, with the purchase of T-shirt in Hawaii that said "Anna's Bannanas." (Yes, the shirt misspelled banana, which makes it even more of a collector's item.) As Ann showed off her shirt, friends started sending her banana collectibles from all over the world, until the collection took on a life of its own. To view the bananarama, call Ann on her banana phone to make an appointment. Her banana enthusiasm is contagious. We're just thankful her extensive collection does not include banana slugs, the enormous mottled yellow and brown slimy creatures indigenous to our region. (Don't get any ideas, Ann!)

WORLD'S LARGEST ROSARY COLLECTION
STEVENSON

Looking at Donald Brown's unfathomable rosary collection, all that comes to mind is *Oh, my God, I've never seen so many rosaries.* Brown has the largest rosary collection in the entire world, and it's right here at the Columbia Gorge Interpretive Center Museum in Stevenson. For those who aren't Catholic, rosaries are strings of prayer beads used in devotions. Madonna converted them into a fashion accessory in the 1980s. But how did 4000 rosaries from all around the world get to be in one place?

The story goes like this: Don Brown was seriously ill as a child, hospitalized with pneumonia. As he lay in his sick bed, he noticed the rosaries worn by the Sisters of Mercy who cared for him. Don recovered and grew up to become a Dominican Brother. He began to collect rosaries. As his collection grew, friends and people he had never met sent him rosaries from across the globe. One was a gift from television personality Lawrence Welk (no, it was not made of bubbles). Lou Holtz, Notre Dame's football coach, sent another. Some were even blessed by the Pope.

But Don's favorite was the wooden rosary John F. Kennedy carried with him during World War II. JFK's wartime prayer beads are on display in the Spiritual Quest exhibit of the museum, along with rosaries made of such diverse materials as glass, bone, ivory, leather, yarn, gemstones, bullets, even olive pits. The largest of the collection is 16 feet long and was made by children— out of Styrofoam. Others are artfully arranged to form an American flag. The collection has been described as a jewel box because of its surprising beauty. Sadly, Brother Brown departed this world in 1975, but the collection he built up over 60 years serves well as a memorial of his life's work.

WASHINGTON SERPENTARIUM
MONROE

Only six zoos in the world have an albino alligator, and one of the specimens is in the Pacific Northwest, at the Washington Serpentarium. The unusual reptile is currently only three years old, and it could live to 100. The proud owner is Scott Petersen, a.k.a. "the Reptile Man," who gained local fame on the TV show *Bill Nye, The Science Guy.* Petersen is something of a reptile whisperer. He understands these creatures, and they seem to show him respect. The Reptile Man recently moved his reptile zoo to a new location, one mile east of the city of Monroe. His serpentarium houses creatures rarely seen elsewhere, such as large

anacondas, a Brazilian pink tarantula, a two-headed turtle, a monkey tail skink and the world's top 10 deadliest snakes, including a green mamba, an Egyptian cobra and a puff adder.

Fear not—all of the venomous snakes have been surgically devenomized, and you can actually hold some of them. Children especially love the creepy crawly aspect, and braver ones dare each other to let a hairy tarantula crawl across their face, a perfectly safe activity under the Reptile Man's supervision.

The Reptile Man uses his teaching credentials to debunk myths about these frequently misunderstood creatures. He even takes his exhibit on the road upon request, bringing his collection to schools and to corporations such as Microsoft and Boeing. But if you prefer to stay on your own side of the glass while the reptiles stay safely tucked away on their side, that's okay, too.

CROSBYANA, GONZAGA UNIVERSITY
SPOKANE

You may remember Bing Crosby from his smooth, dulcet rendition of *White Christmas*. But the folks of Spokane remember him as their hometown boy who made it big. Bing's alma mater, Gonzaga University, has devoted an entire campus room in the student union to Bing Crosby memorabilia. It's called Crosbyana. The miniature museum showcases Bing's platinum and gold records, photographs and music, along with the Academy Award he received for Best Actor in 1944 for *Going My Way*. It also

includes some unusual finds, such as a Bing Crosby "Call
Me Lucky" board game and a Bing Crosby ice cream carton.
Thanks to a generous gift from Crosby, the house he grew up
in is an unofficial part of the collection. The house is near the
university and now serves as the Gonzaga Alumni Association.
The collection continues in the home, and you can almost hear
the voice of young Bing echoing in the hall, saying something
about making show biz history one day.

AMERICAN HOP MUSEUM
TOPPENISH

Amsterdam has its Hash Museum, and New York has the Museum
of Sex. But this is Washington, and we've got the American Hop
Museum, because if there's anything more popular in America
than hash or sex, it's beer. The museum is the only one of its
kind in the country, located right in the heart of the nation's
largest hop-producing area, Yakima Valley. The valley supplies

most of the hops in the U.S., which in turn makes up about one-quarter of the hops in the world. This farming industry is big business, but the museum brings hops back to its roots.

Even the building that houses the museum is a living piece of hop history, the lovingly restored old Hop Growers Supply building. Inside, museum exhibits trace the history of the hop industry from the vine's humble beginnings in the New England colonies to its explosion out to the West to its increased popularity. The museum preserves historical artifacts and equipment such as antique hop presses and cast iron stoves from the 1800s, a horse-drawn hop duster and quality vintage photos and publications. Yakima Valley's own hop memorabilia is also featured. For a solid dose of local history and industry, hop over to the hop museum—and don't miss the "Hoptoberfest" held each October!

WORLD KITE MUSEUM AND HALL OF FAME
(AND INTERNATIONAL KITE FESTIVAL)
LONG BEACH

Aw, go fly a kite! No, really! This is the place to do it! The only kite museum in North America is in Long Beach. The American Kite Association combined its archives with the town's local museum to form a complete history of kites, kite makers and the people who fly them. The World Kite Museum and Hall of Fame houses 1500 kites, including the David Checkley Asian Kite Collection, considered the most complete collection of Japanese kites outside Japan.

The museum is as educational as it is entertaining. It turns out that kites aren't just child's play. An in-depth exhibit of the kite's 2000-year history examines how kites have been used in times of war. In the Civil War, for example, the Union Army used

kites to drop leaflets encouraging the Confederates to surrender. In World War II, the military employed kites for communication, before it had radar. The museum also offers lighthearted fun. Children and adults alike get to play with the exhibits and enjoy hands-on workshops.

The museum's efforts culminate in the Washington State International Kite Festival, a celebration and competition held for an entire week each August, which was voted the Best Kite Festival in the World by Kite Trade Association International. Kite flyers and enthusiasts come from all over the world for a giant mass ascension that takes over the sky, transforming it into a sea of color and whimsy.

EXPERIENCE MUSIC PROJECT
SEATTLE

You can't miss the Experience Music Project (EMP). Right underneath the Space Needle in Seattle Center, in a sea of gray and green nature tones, the psychedelic, wavy Frank Gehry building screams, "Look at me!" It's hard not to. Visitors are alternately thrilled and puzzled, asking each other, what is *that* supposed to be? The answer: a smashed guitar, Jimi Hendrix style. Art or eyesore—you be the judge.

The EMP, a unique rock 'n' roll museum, has changed Seattle's landscape in more ways than one. Museums were once thought to be formal, stuffy affairs, with harsh warnings of "Do not touch!" This museum, however, is hands-on, encouraging visitors to play, experiment and *experience* the music (get it?). The Sound Lab's electric guitars, drums, microphones and keyboards unleash your inner rock star, and you can even record your own CD. Interactive exhibits teach you how to play "Louie, Louie" and how to scratch a record like a real hip-hop DJ. Soundproof pods offer privacy as you rehearse. You can try out a private recording studio, or step into the spotlight and pretend you're on *American Idol.* The museum also lets you create a video complete with (pre-recorded) screaming fans to take home.

The accessibility of the music is one of the best parts of visiting EMP. The other is that you get to enjoy all of Paul Allen's pricey toys. He founded the museum with his own collection of rock memorabilia. In it, he pays tribute to Northwest music icons, including Kurt Cobain and Nirvana, Pearl Jam, Quincy Jones, Heart, Soundgarden, The Kingsmen and The Ventures. The EMP also hosts the Sky Church, in honor of Seattle native Jimi Hendrix who dreamed of a place where artists could come together to exchange ideas and make music. That dream lives on at the EMP. And if that's not cool enough for you, the Seattle monorail goes right through the building!

CHIMPANZEE AND HUMAN COMMUNICATION INSTITUTE
ELLENSBERG

Central Washington University (CWU) offers an entirely unique educational experience—and you don't even have to go back to college. The Chimpanzee and Human Communication Institute (CHCI) is part of the university in Ellensburg, where it teaches chimpanzees American Sign Language (ASL). CHCI is the first and longest-running research project of its kind, studying primate communication among chimps as well as between them and humans. The institute serves as a training center for CWU students and offers "chimposiums" to educate the public. But it's not a zoo, and the chimps are not there to perform for you or to entertain you. The staff is quite clear about that; the institute is the chimps' home.

Three of the chimpanzees—Tatu, 33; Dar, 32; and Loulis, 30—live at CHCI full time, rescued from scientific research. Their life at the institute mimics free living in the African jungle. The main difference is their education and ability to sign. The oldest chimpanzee in the program, Washoe, age 43, was raised from infancy and was immersed in ASL, which she soon learned to use to communicate with her human caretakers. All four of these chimpanzees now have extensive ASL vocabularies. They gesture to humans, to each other and "talk" to themselves when alone. They even sign in their sleep.

Observing their conversations, researchers have learned that the chimpanzees communicate the way humans do (not surprising, since they share 98.76% of our DNA). The chimps can even go back and correct themselves and make up through language when they have a misunderstanding. They have also illustrated an ability to create new words for newly introduced objects. When they were introduced to a watermelon, for example, a word for which they had not yet been taught a name, they combined two signs to describe what they saw, creating a new word "drink fruit." In addition, the chimpanzees have demonstrated the ability to teach sign language to each other; Baby Loulis learned to sign from his mother.

Chimposiums offer the opportunity to play Jane Goodall for a day, observing the chimps as they go about their business and eavesdropping on their conversations. If you're lucky, they may initiate a conversation with you—they've been known to "speak" to visitors through the window on occasion. Chimposiums range from a one-hour visit to a five-hour workshop.

The workshop is a full-fledged class in chimpanzee culture and conservation (did you know that chimps are an endangered species, with only about 110,000 left on the planet?). It includes a guided observation of the chimpanzee family, and the chance to eat dinner with them. Sort of. They have to stay behind their glass, but you do dine at the same time and observe them eating on camera. (Because chimps are so much stronger than humans, no visitors are permitted within the enclosure.) One Chimposium alum says of her experience: "It was amazing to be able to see the chimpanzees signing and interacting with us and each other…We really felt like we were entering their world." If you're intrigued, but can't get there in person, you can still observe the chimps via a "chimpcam" on the organization's website.

WOLF HAVEN
TENINO

The wolves at Wolf Haven don't sign, but the organization shares the same principles of wildlife conservation and education as CHCI. Wolf Haven is the only private wolf sanctuary in the United States. The non-profit organization has rescued more than 100 captive-born wolves since 1982. Gray wolves, red wolves, coyotes, wolf-dog hybrids and a few foxes have found a permanent home among 80 acres of nature. The sanctuary

also does its part for conservation—it is one of only three pre-release breeding facilities in the country working to re-establish the southwestern Mexican gray wolf population.

Wolf Haven commits to the lifetime protection and care of its resident wolves. But the keepers do more than let wolves be wolves; they educate the public about wolf behavior, encouraging respect for the animals' wild nature. Visitors can explore the peaceful Mima prairie and native vegetation independently, but the only way to see the wolves is by a guided walking tour. In less than an hour, the tour covers the basics of wolf biology, along with Wolf Haven's rescue and recovery efforts and the personal history of some of the wolves you might encounter. The sanctuary also sponsors a Wolf Awareness Week, Howl-o-ween events and family Howl-Ins with optional overnight camping on Wolf Haven's grounds. No, you can't feed the wolves.

OLYMPIC GAME FARM
SEQUIM

On the other end of the spectrum, Olympic Game Farm invites you to "get face to face with wildlife." And they do mean face to face. If you don't go to the animals, they'll come to you, like the buffalo that nosed his way into my friend's car window to offer a slobbery hello. The Olympic Game Farm animals are very outgoing. Many of them are performing animals with Hollywood resumes. Walt Disney Studios filmed them right at the farm from 1962 to the early 1970s. The animals have appeared in nearly 100 movies, including the original *The Incredible Journey*. Sets from many of their films are on display in the Farm's Studio Barn, made from one of the oldest trees on the Olympic Peninsula. Although the popularity of nature films eventually waned, the show goes on at the farm, where the animals play to an appreciative audience.

At the Olympic Game Farm, the animals roam free—you're the one captive in your car. Think of it as a Washington safari. You can opt for the popular drive-through tour, or you can get out and greet the animals on foot. Both tours start with a loaf of bread so you can hand-feed your new friends, which are surprisingly gentle. Next come the performing bears—a Mommy and Me duo so sweet your teeth will hurt. The farm also has a rare white rhinoceros, tigers, zebras, llamas, elk, yaks and black-tailed prairie dogs, along with endangered species such as Bengal tigers, African lions and timber wolves. This is animal watching at its best.

HYDROPLANE AND RACEBOAT MUSEUM
KENT

Hydroplane racing is a big deal in western Washington. Seattle is considered the hydro capital of the world. The city hosts the Chevrolet Cup Hydroplane Races on Lake Washington, a focal point of the annual Seafair celebration. The Hydroplane and Raceboat Museum says the races draw a bigger audience than any Seahawks, Sonics or Mariners game, and that's saying a lot.

The nation's only public museum devoted to powerboat racing, the museum preserves and exhibits vintage hydroplanes, including boats that have won a total of 17 Gold Cups. It also serves as the primary resource for archival materials on hydroplane racing, including historical documents, programs, photos, trophies and artifacts that date back to the 1916 American Power Boat Association (APBA) Gold Cup. The museum brings new participants up to speed by sharing rare film footage of races from the 1940s to the present. Exhibits honor the men behind the machines, from legendary driver "Wild" Bill Cantrell to modern favorite Chip Hanauer.

The museum not only preserves raceboat history, but it also makes it in a boat restoration shop. The shop is responsible for bringing seven of the top Gold Cup and Harmsworth winners back to life and into full running condition. Fans will recognize the 1929s *Miss America VIII, Slo-mo-shun IV* and *V,* and the famous *Green Dragon. Miss Budweiser* 1967 sounds like a beauty queen, and she is, except that she's a boat. *Miss Budweiser* set a new world record for racing at a speed of 220.493 miles per hour. You can sidle up to this dreamboat in the museum or even join the volunteer crew that restores these beauties. It's no wonder the museum has been called a Disneyland for big boat fans.

MUSEUM OF GLASS
TACOMA

The Museum of Glass gives Tacoma a claim to fame *besides* the aroma of Tacoma. For those not from around here, Tacoma is Washington state's third largest municipality, and it gets a lot of flack from neighboring cities (you know who you are, Seattle!) for the odor created by the city's paper mill. It smells a bit like rotten eggs (or worse). Thankfully, now that the Museum of Glass International Center for Contemporary Art is here, people have something else to talk about. This innovative museum aims to make Tacoma a hip destination, with its swanky modern building and catchy slogan: "Hot glass. Cool art."

The museum is the brainchild of famous glass artist Dale Chihuly. You'd know him if you saw him—he's the curly-haired character wearing an eye patch, whose stunning glass art is everywhere in Washington (not to mention museums all over the world). He was actually the first person to be named a United States Living National Treasure. Chihuly was born in Tacoma, and as the local success story, he wanted to give something back to his hometown. So he created the Bridge of Glass, a $12-million structure linking the Museum of Glass to downtown Tacoma. Says Chihuly, "The bridge is the gateway that

welcomes people to Tacoma. We wanted something unique in the world, something that is full of color and offers a joyous experience to passersby both night and day."

The joyous experience is provided by Chihuly himself, whose vibrant glassworks line the bridge, illuminating it with vivid color and warmth—500 feet of brilliant, renowned art permanently on display for the public to enjoy. Follow the bridge to the museum and you'll find it a step above the usual. The Museum of Glass is downright cutting edge, offering podcasts to accompany your visit, instead of the usual stale headset recording. The exhibits feature distinguished contemporary glass artists. They also show you how it's done at an amphitheater hot shop, where molten glass is transformed into art right before your eyes. Items made at the museum can be purchased and brought home as a memento.

CARR'S ONE OF A KIND MUSEUM
SPOKANE

Marvin Carr is an eccentric. He serves as tour guide of an eclectic private museum he describes as "a million dollar slice of American history." The highlight of the museum is Carr's cars, which were previously owned by celebrities. There is a certain novelty to sitting in Elvis Presley's 1973 Lincoln Mark IV while the King's voice croons in the background. Sitting where Elvis sat is sort of like your backside vicariously touching his through time. Carr also displays Jackie Gleason's powder blue 1968 limo, and President John F. Kennedy's personal 1962 Lincoln Continental (which Carr purports met Marilyn Monroe on more than one occasion).

Once you leave the classic cars, though, the museum gets spotty and downright odd. There's a Navy destroyer, the skin carcass of an electrocuted 13-foot snake, a model ship made of 27,500 matchsticks and a host of other random items, some of which look like plain old junk. But, hey, if you're looking for weird and wacky, Carr's museum definitely qualifies.

ROSALIE WHYEL MUSEUM OF DOLL ART
BELLEVUE

This doll museum isn't just for youngsters. The Rosalie Whyel Museum of Doll Art is a hub of the collectors' world, and a winner of the prestigious Jumeau Trophy for Best Private Doll Museum in the World. The pretty pink building is a dollhouse in itself, complete with an English garden and Victorian elegance. Little girls use the facility for birthday tea parties, and "big girls" rent it for fairytale weddings.

More than 1200 dolls are displayed at the museum, from 17th-century miniatures to Mattel's first Barbie from 1959. Dolls are celebrated as an art form and as permanent portraits of history. In addition to the bisque china beauties you'd expect to find, the collection includes some notable surprises: an Alaskan Inuit doll made of ivory and adorned with tribal facial tattoos, an Iranian wax figure, a male Japanese doll created from ground oyster shells and the Michael Langton's original sailor-suited Elmer. Plush teddy bears, elaborate dollhouses and childhood memorabilia round out the museum, which also has a gift shop so you can add to your own collection. From the cloyingly cute to the curious, the doll museum appeals to all ages.

YE OLDE CURIOSITY SHOP
SEATTLE

Honestly now, who among us isn't curious enough to want to check out Siamese-twin calves; Ecuadorian shrunken heads; mummified, murdered prospectors; jack rabbits with antelope antlers and the like? We humans are equally revolted and attracted by the macabre, and the best place to check out a great many of the world's oddities is at the Ye Olde Curiosity Shop on Seattle's Pier 54. The "shop" first opened in 1899 as a "Museum of Natural Wonders," but over time it's evolved into a museum and novelty shop (where you can actually buy a shrunken head if you're so inclined).

Since the late J.E. "Daddy" Standley first opened the doors of his famous shop, he and his descendants have scoured the world in search of collections of oddities being auctioned off here or there to add to their own burgeoning assortment of artifacts. In a *Seattle Times* article heralding the shop's 100th birthday in July 1999, Standley's grandson, 75-year-old Joe James, told how his grandfather "was a curio-lover first and a businessman second."

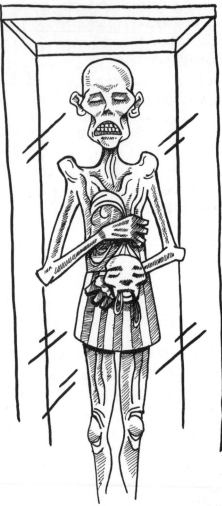

The mix proved to be a good one, though, in that the business has thrived, providing a century and more of visitors with something to talk about. Although admission is free, Standley believed that a person's curiosity would draw them into the shop and, after they spent some time there, they wouldn't be able to leave without picking up a little something to commemorate their visit. He must have been right—a great many patrons make repeat visits over the years. Among the more elite clientele to cross the threshold of Ye Olde Curiosity Shop in search of other-worldly mysteries are Theodore Roosevelt, Katharine Hepburn and John Wayne. Robert Ripley of "Ripley's Believe It or Not" called it "the greatest shop I ever got into."

MARSH'S FREE MUSEUM
LONG BEACH

Back when I was a youngster, I had the unfortunate experience of peeking around the corner of my family's living room entry-way (when I was supposed to be fast asleep, of course). What I saw on that snowy, static-ridden, black-and-white TV screen haunted my dreams for many years to come, and when I caught a glimpse of Jake the Alligator Man at Marsh's Free Museum, that earlier memory was once more refreshed. The horror movie I wasn't supposed to see showed a man being transformed into a King Cobra. Marsh's Free Museum seems to have its own variation on the B-rated flick with mummified Jake the Alligator Man—the half-alligator, half-human immortalized in tabloid headlines. The only difference is that Jake was supposedly a real "thing" in his day, apparently escorting men in search of a little lovin' to their rooms in a New Orleans brothel—which has

a wall full of tabloid newspaper clippings to prove it! Jake has the familiar head and torso of a human, but the lower body of an alligator—complete with tail. His withered hands are like little claws, and his eyes have dried to mere slits, but he's recognizable as the famous Jake from postcards. He has established his own fan base.

But Jake isn't the only oddity you'll find at this out-of-the ordinary museum. In the spirit of Ye Olde Curiosity Shop, Marsh's Free Museum in Long Beach boasts its own bizarre assortment of the odd and macabre, including the obligatory shrunken heads, two-headed calves, eight-legged lambs and a collection of petrified dinosaur dung.

The evolution of this museum is almost as odd as its beginnings. It started out as a candy shop and ice cream parlor when Wellington Marsh Sr. first opened his enterprise in the early 1930s, and by 1937 it had become Marsh's Seashell Factory and Antiques which, after another few decades, evolved into the museum you see today.

GIANT SHOE MUSEUM
SEATTLE

When it comes to weird and wacky tourist attractions, the Giant Shoe Museum in Seattle's Pike Place Market has to be among the most bizarre. Although it doesn't have shrunken heads or man-alligators, it has two things that even the most stoic person finds alluring—mystery and a story. Let's start with the story.

Back in 1938, Robert Wadlow—the world's largest man, in case you weren't on a first name basis—was touring the countryside promoting products for the International Shoe Company. It is a no-brainer that with a height of 8 feet, 11.1 inches, and weighing in at 490 pounds, this guy needed a pretty big pair of shoes to accommodate his equally large feet. While in Seattle, Robert apparently had a pair of shoes, size 37, that were in need of

repair, and he brought them to a shoe store located in Pike Place Market. Somehow Robert ended up leaving before retrieving the shoes, or perhaps they needed to be sent out and were to be mailed to him once the repairs were completed. Either way, Robert didn't have his shoes, and when he returned to inquire about them, they seemed to have disappeared.

Being an enterprising sort of fellow, the shop owner at the time advertised for the missing shoes and received quite a response. A veritable flood of extra-large footwear, including another pair belonging to Robert, descended on him, but the pair that started it all was still missing.

Fast-forward to 1976, where there's a pile of old, used, plus-sized shoes, and the original shoe shop has either moved or gone out of business. That's when John Hanawalt opens up his Old Seattle Paperworks in the same location in Pike Place Market. While most of us would have likely pitched the shoe collection and washed our hands with disinfectant soap, John had a more inventive idea. He proposed that he give up one-third of his shop's window space for a unique display dedicated to the world's largest shoes, of which he was obviously in possession. After a fair bit of haggling with the Pike Place Historical Commission, John's idea to open the Giant Shoe Museum was finally a go.

For the price of four quarters, you get to peek in the window four times. Each quarter inserted into a coin box raises a curtain directly in front of the window (we all know everyone wants to see what's behind a closed curtain) and briefly displays a pair of giant clown shoes, Robert Wadlow wingtips and whatever other super-sized footwear happens to be behind it. But you'd better pay close attention, because the curtain doesn't stay up for long, and it'll cost you another quarter for a second look!

NUTCRACKER MUSEUM
LEAVENWORTH

Okay. I confess. I had no idea the complexities involved in the development of the nutcracker, but after touring through the Leavenworth Nutcracker Museum, I have a new appreciation for the instrument. The seed of interest that eventually blossomed into this one-of-a-kind museum began with owner Arlene Wagner's other love, ballet. As a teacher, she'd choreographed students through the Nutcracker Ballet many times over and eventually, it wasn't just the ballet that captured her heart but the nutcracker as well.

Whenever she and her husband, George, traveled, they'd often purchase a nutcracker as a souvenir. Over time, the couple accumulated more than 5000 nutcrackers from more than 40 countries, ranking their collection as one of the largest of its kind in the world. And when a collection gets as large as that, it's obvious a museum to house and share the collection with others must be established.

The Leavenworth Nutcracker Museum opened its doors in 1995 and has hosted visitors from "44 states and 38 foreign countries." Aside from viewing the vast collection, visitors are taken through the history of the instrument, from its conception to the first awkward models (including a 2000-year-old Roman nutcracker), to a display of nutcracker oddities (ranging from the screw-variety of nutcrackers to nut-cracking shoes) available today. The nutcrackers are made of everything from ivory to bronze to wood. You'll also learn how the lingo has changed throughout the years—they used to call nutcrackers "nut biters" because they opened nuts by biting down on them. So if you're in Leavenworth one day and feeling a little nutty, a stop at the Nutcracker Museum is a must!

RUSSIAN COBRA
SEATTLE

Come on, admit it. All you James Bond fans out there are just itching to take a trip to Seattle. And for those of you who aren't sure why that might be, listen up. Safely secured on Pier 48 of Seattle's waterfront is the Russian *Foxtrot* submarine, codename *Cobra*. It measures 284 feet in length, and in its day, it could accommodate 56 sailors, 10 midshipmen and 12 officers. The submarine, which was built in the Sudomekh Shipyard in Leningrad, could travel at speeds of 15 knots and was in operation from 1974 to 1994.

Although the rule of the sea is one country's ships and subs shouldn't get too close to another's, there are times when that rule is bent or even broken. That appears to have been the case with the *Cobra*. After all, it is docked on American soil, but it didn't get there through a too-close encounter at sea. Actually, the sub was decommissioned, and obviously sold, though how it eventually made its way to Seattle isn't at all clear.

Nonetheless, a tour of the sub gives you a firsthand look at life under the sea, the living quarters of the sailors and officers, the ins and outs of armament, and more. Of course, if you're the claustrophobic sort, it might be a little too cozy for you.

VINTAGE MOTORCYCLE MUSEUM
CHEHALIS

There's something about men and their vehicles. Be they four-wheelers or the two-wheel kind, it appears that owning one machine on wheels is simply not enough for some men. It's as if a built-in drive propels these men into buying one or two or a few more.

Frank Mason first started collecting motorcycles back in the 1970s as a way to relax from his seven-day-a-week contracting business. His wife, Barb, likely thought he'd buy one or two motorcycles to tinker with in the family's garage, and things would stop there.

Ha ha! Not so! Mr. Mason was so enamored with his new hobby (some would call it an obsession) that he kept buying more and more motorcycles, supplementing them with a collection of bicycles. Eventually he had so many prime examples of bikes, predominantly dating to 1916 and earlier, that it was a sin not to share them with the rest of the world.

That's when Frank decided to buy a 6000-square-foot, two-story building in Chehalis' historic downtown and set up the Vintage Motorcycle Museum. (His wife must have breathed a sign of relief.) Using his skills in construction, he refurbished the old building, bringing it back to its former glory. Stopping by for a visit is a must, even if motorbikes aren't your passion, because his display really gives visitors a chance to see how the transportation industry evolved from its earliest designs.

Among his wide assortment of models, Mason also has Harley, Excelsior, Indian and Sears models; one and two-seater varieties of bikes; and even a 1908 Indian Tri-Car that, to an untrained eye, looks more like a bicycle pushing a wheelchair than a motorized bike. Mason's collection also boasts an Amphi Car—a land and water vehicle that was experimented with in the 1960s but never really made much of a splash, except the movie varieties used in Bond films.

TUNNEL TREE
ARLINGTON

If you live in an area where wispy willows or silver birch are the norm, it might be hard to fathom a tree with a trunk that's large enough to drive through. But Arlington was once home to just such a tree. Depending on the source, the western red cedar lovingly known to residents as the Giant Cedar Stump is believed to be somewhere between 1250 and 2000 years old, and though its preservation has been a prime concern with area residents throughout the years, the stump has been moved several times.

It was first made famous by renowned photographer Darius Kinsey. He initially photographed the stump back in 1901, by which time it had already sported a peaked roof and a hollowed-out center large enough for a car to drive through. Currently, the Giant Cedar Stump can be found at a rest area on I-5, northbound, near mile marker 207. Just don't try and drive through it—these days it's open to pedestrian traffic only.

GREAT WALL OF WASHINGTON
RUBY HILL

The actual reasoning behind the building of what some in the state call the "China Wall" seems shrouded in mystery. Most sources do agree, however, that the mastermind behind a series of granite walls was a mining entrepreneur named Jonathan Bourne. Bourne was a lawyer from Oregon with a taste for precious metals, and in 1888 he used some of his considerable inheritance to buy up 27 mining claims near Ruby Hill in Loup Loup country. He then set out to build the Arlington Mill and, along with it, a series of 10 walls. The longest of these walls measures 80 feet in length and is 27 feet high, and in some places the walls are almost 3 feet thick. Altogether, the walls stretch for an impressive 800 feet.

Sadly, Bourne's hope for a mining empire never materialized. The mill went bankrupt in 1889, before it was even open for business. Today, all that remains of Bourne's dreams are the walls. They are located about 5 miles from the Rock Creek Campground, but if you're planning to check it out, be prepared. Road conditions near the wall are reported to be in poor condition.

Freaky Festivals

Washington traditions are full of contradictions. People are generally so law-abiding that jaywalking is regarded as a heinous crime, yet we honor a legendary skyjacker every November, and locals re-enact a horseback robbery in Oakville each July. We're a gentle people—our Seafair pirates do charity work and cheer up children in local hospitals—but we're not afraid of controversy either, or bodily harm. Washington is the only place in the country where the dangerous tradition of extreme horseracing lives on.

We do crazy things, such as rescuing old combines and then smashing them up in a single afternoon. We race everything from speedboats to outhouses to beds. And we don't complain about the sometimes foot-long slimy banana slugs that invade our gardens and sidewalks; instead, we throw a festival in their honor, because, well, they're part of what makes our home unique. If there's one thing we love, it's a celebration.

MARCHING TO A DIFFERENT DRUMMER

THE LAST HORSEBACK BANK ROBBERY RE-ENACTMENT
OAKVILLE

What is it with historical re-enactments? Back east they re-enact Civil War battles. Here in the tiny timber town of Oakville, they recreate the last great horse robbery. Oakville's big moment in history was in the 1930s or '40s (no one remembers the exact year), when its corner bank was robbed by an armed man who used a horse for his getaway ride. The ensuing shootout left a bullet hole in the bank building that's still there. That was the last Washington state bank robbery on horseback, a dubious honor the town celebrates to this day.

Each year, Oakville's Fourth of July celebration and parade culminates in a staged robbery with costumed horseback contestants.

Volunteers erect a makeshift bank front at the original scene of the crime (now a Sterling Savings Bank) and watch, applauding, as their bank gets robbed again and again. Current bank employees gleefully hand the masked bandits bags stuffed with fake bills. There's even a prize for the best re-enactment skit, determined by audience applause. Contestants range from legitimate horse-riding club members to local children playing make-believe on brooms and mops. The winning group receives a plaque of distinction and a check for real, cold hard cash from Sterling Savings Bank. A crowd of nearly 200 people observes the annual tradition, and actual robberies have not increased as a result. It's just good old-fashioned horseplay—so much fun it's almost criminal.

D.B. COOPER DAYS
ARIEL

On Thanksgiving eve, November 24, 1971, Dan Cooper (a.k.a. D.B. Cooper) hijacked a Boeing 727 flying from Portland to Seattle. Claiming his briefcase contained a bomb, Cooper demanded and received $200,000 in ransom money (and four parachutes) from the FBI. He jumped out of the plane with the cash somewhere over the town of Ariel in Cowlitz County and was never seen again. Ariel General Store and Tavern hosts D.B. Cooper Days every November in honor of the world's only unsolved hijacking—and Ariel's only claim to fame. Back in the day, this tiny town on Lake Merwin helped search for Cooper. They never found him, but that doesn't stop them from continuing to try, and continuing to celebrate this quirky moment in Washington history. Up to 500 fans of the mystery attend each year to participate in a D.B. Cooper look-a-like contest and a D.B. Cooper anthem sing-along (the song, by Richard Purdy, is on the tavern's jukebox). Revelers tell stories and share theories in Ariel Store's "Cooper Corner," an unofficial mini-museum filled with yellowing articles about the unsolved case. The party is always held on the Saturday after Thanksgiving, near the anniversary of Cooper's plunge.

A major break in the case was the discovery of $5800 in ransom money, all in ragged $20 bills, found by a boy near the Columbia River in 1980. Investigators doubt Cooper survived the 10,000-foot jump in the dark and rain, but because his real identity is unknown, the case remains open. Public interest was rekindled in March 2008, when two young boys found a white parachute half-buried in the dirt in the town of Amboy, 20 miles south of Ariel. While the FBI investigates whether the tattered chute could be Cooper's, Ariel Store is making parachute-themed T-shirts for this year's D.B. Cooper Days. Maybe Cooper will show up at his own party at Ariel Store. Better keep an eye out at that look-a-like contest...

THE TESTICLE FESTIVAL AND COWBOY CAVIAR FETE

CONCONULLY

While gourmet restaurants crowd big cities like Seattle, the town of Conconully, population 200, hosts the Testicle Festival and Cowboy Caviar Fete contest in homage to the prairie cowboy delicacy of bull testicles. The town's only three restaurants— Sit'n Bull (you can't make this stuff up...), The Tamarack, and Lucky D's—cook up a competition in which the tastiest morsels win... a "Balls to the Wall" award. It's similar to a specialty version of TV's *Top Chef* (or, given the ingredients, some might say *Hell's Kitchen*). Local versions of Rocky Mountain oysters range from cowboy caviar on the half shell and skewered shish-ke-balls, to, goodness gracious, Great "Balls of Fire" (apologies to Jerry Lee Lewis). The Tamarack even serves up Hawaiian flair, adorning sliced testicles with sweet 'n' sour pineapple. What, no miniature umbrella? (Give 'em time, folks.)

The foodie approach to gourmet gonads began in 2003. Apparently the annual Outhouse Races weren't enough entertainment for this small town, so they added a culinary festival. One day, local farmers were discussing calf castration, that unkindest cut that separates a bull from a steer, and, well, the idea presented itself. Now, each June, people travel from all over to taste the testes. The event sells about 300 tickets a year, 1.5 times the town's population! Ten dollars buys "ball-you-can-eat" and the opportunity to vote for your favorite.

Of course, no party is complete without royalty, so the festival also selects a king and queen of the ball. In 2005, the honor was auctioned off on eBay, where it sold for $1225 to an online casino. More recently, however, the town has returned to its rural roots, bestowing the titles by lottery. This ball may be a little nutty, but it did help put Conconully on the map.

OUTHOUSE RACES
CONCONULLY

Between the Testicle Festival and the Outhouse Races, Conconully is a contender for Washington's strangest small town. February 2008 marked the 25th anniversary of its Annual Outhouse Races. Washington's races may not be as big as the famous Outhouse Classic in northern Michigan, but they are the longest running.

Every year for the past 25 years, more than 100 contestants have raced homemade wooden outhouses down a single block slope on Main Street. The jostling johns are all mounted on a single pair of skis, with two team members pushing the privy while one rider sits on the throne. According to the rules, each outhouse must be equipped with a toilet seat and toilet paper, and all riders must wear helmets. The terrain can be rough—sometimes there's snow and ice—but no one has ever been hurt, not even in the most challenging division of bucket racing. Bucket racers literally place a bucket over their heads and guide the outhouse blind, while the racer perched on the toilet seat remains bucketless and hollers out directions. It's a hoot to watch. Teams also decorate their outhouses with pride, kind of like the Red Bull Soap Box Derby in Seattle, but more home-spun. The event awards prizes and division championships to creatively named teams, which have included The King's Throne and The General Pee.

SEAFAIR
SEATTLE

When I first moved to Seattle, I didn't know anything about Seafair. I arrived days before Seattle's biggest summer celebra-tion, and I remember riding downtown on the bus when a band of pirates whizzed by on a makeshift float. Some of them jumped out at the stoplight to approach our windows. I assumed they were a gang and we were about to be mugged. But it was just the pirates from Seafair. To know them is to love them.

The band of 40 Seafair pirates has been swashbuckling since 1949, and the scallywags take it very seriously. Behind their swinging swords, blackened teeth and loud cries of "Arrgh," these pirates hide hearts of gold. They host more than 100 charity events a year, visit sick children in hospitals, amuse old folks in nursing homes and commit themselves to community service. They also add a splash of local color to the annual Seafair.

Seafair officially launches with the Pirates Landing at Alki Beach in West Seattle. Thousands crowd the beach to await the arrival of the pirates' flagship Moby Duck, a surplus World War II truck equipped with a small cannon. The cannon blasts, the pirates storm the beach in an explosion of scallywag shenanigans, and Seafair has begun.

Seafair's five-week festival is the largest in the Northwest, with more than two million people attending each summer. The alfresco festival culminates in the Blue Angels air show and hydroplane races on Lake Washington, and also encompasses the popular Milk Carton Derby, the Seafair fleet arrival and the Torchlight Run and Parade. Seafair inspires additional neighborhood and cultural events of every kind, from an Indian Days Powwow to a Ballard Seafoodfest.

Seafair all started with Seattle's centennial in 1951–52. The first Seafair was created to highlight Seattle's claim as the "boating capital of the world." Hydroplane racing captured the heart of Seattle in 1950 when the *Slo-mo-shun IV* broke the world record for speed on water. The Unlimited Hydroplane Races continue today as high-speed hydroplanes thunder across Lake Washington, competing for the Chevrolet Cup.

Meanwhile, up above, the famous U.S. Navy Blue Angels Flight Demonstration Squadron takes over the sky. This spectacular show of aerial acrobatics has become synonymous with Seafair and is the definite highlight. The Blue Angels perform the ultimate in precision flying. The choreographed planes seem to dance overhead, first graceful and elegant, then low and fast with sudden vertical rolls, until finally all six jets move in breathtakingly perfect Delta formation. The Air Force gets in on the act, too, with fly-bys of planes such as the B-52 Bomber and C-141 Starlifter. The U.S. Marine Corps performs a thrilling Harrier demonstration, where the jet comes to a complete stop mid-flight.

The hydroplane race isn't the only boat race during Seafair. Folks without race boats can still compete in the annual Milk Carton Derby, in which homemade watercraft made from 50-plus-gallon milk cartons float across 1200 feet of Green Lake. Between 60 and 100 handcrafted boats compete in front of 25,000 spectators who watch from the shoreline. Boats must be exclusively human-powered and rely only on the milk cartons for floatation. Some of them are actually quite pretty and detailed, such as the giant, yellow, non-rubber duckie named "Duck Amuck." She won the prize for Grand Showboat in 2007. Creativity rules at this competition—whatever floats your boat.

Seattle's largest parade, the Torchlight Parade, draws crowds of 300,000 spectators each year, some of whom arrive the night before with a blanket and cooler to secure a good spot. It's the grand finale of a five-week series of parades, all hosted by Seafair. The Torchlight Parade begins at dusk and encourages participants to get creative when illuminating their floats. The resulting lightshow is a spectacle of giant balloons, elaborate floats, award-winning drill teams, marching bands and cultural dance and performances (such as the beautiful, vibrant Chinese Dragon dance). The parade starts at the Seattle Center and continues all the way to Qwest Field, 2.5 miles downtown.

Those who aren't at the parade in person can be there in spirit: half a million viewers tune in for the live broadcast on television. The parade is preceded by the popular 8k Torchlight Run, which attracts some participants in costume. Miss Seafair, King Neptune and the King's Prime Minister reign over this Seattle treasure and serve as Seafair Royalty, representing the community and promoting the Torchlight Parade and the Seafair festival.

AW SHUCKS! IT'S OYSTERFEST
SHELTON

Never mind the cautionary old wives' tale that states you should only eat oysters in months that contain an "r." That directive stems from an antiquated law that 250 years ago prohibited harvesting oysters on the East Coast during the summer months, when oysters spawn. Spawning oysters don't taste as good anyway—they're too soft and creamy—but refrigeration and transportation challenges are a thing of the past. Modern hatchery techniques have evolved to the point where Seattle's famous "Oyster Bill" Whitbeck of Taylor Shellfish says that as long as you get oysters from a reputable shellfish dealer, you can eat them year-round. One especially entertaining place to do just that is Shelton, which presents its own OysterFest each year during the first weekend of October.

Since 1981, folks in that neck of the woods have been challenging each other to oyster-shucking contests in which competitors pop oysters open and remove them from their shells as fast as possible. Speed, neatness and the condition of the oysters are all taken into consideration. But that's only a part of the excitement. What is an oyster festival without a mouth-watering feast? Alongside the vendors serving up variations of the delicacy, the OysterFest Seafood Cook-Off adds to the aromatic heaven. The cook-off is open to professional and amateur cooks, but being a pro doesn't mean you're a shoe-in for a prize—since the first cook-off, amateurs have captured about 50 percent of the winnings. If you're not into shucking, cooking or eating oysters, there's still an art and photography competition. Even vendors have a chance of being recognized with the "People's Choice—Best of Vendor" award. Amid this sea of superlatives, Shelton's OysterFest emerges as a pearl.

SLUG FEST
EATONVILLE

To live in Washington is to live with slugs. They're everywhere, as attracted as we are to our lush, green, and yes, damp, environment. Twenty-three different species exist on the state's coast. Slugs have been around since dinosaurs roamed the earth, and they show no signs of going extinct. So if you can't beat 'em, join 'em—or at least hold a festival for 'em.

Once upon a time, the little town of Elma hosted a three-day annual Slug Festival in which locals supposedly dressed up slugs in little costumes, and dressed themselves up as slugs, and had races for the title of the Fastest Slug in the State of Washington. The Children's Theater Association even put on musical revues with names such as "Dances with Slugs." (And they say nobody's

heard of Elma.) According to at least one Elma native, after a paltry few years, the town elders decided the event did not portray the ideal image of the small community, so they replaced it with the more likeable Blackberry Festival (yawn). But never fear, the Slug Festival survives in a loud and proud version hosted by Northwest Trek Wildlife Park, where slugs are slugs, and people love them.

The Northwest Trek Wildlife Park in Eatonville sprawls 723 acres, so they have a lot of slugs. The park also has a signature tram tour through an enormous free-roaming habitat where more than 200 animals run wild. Northwest Trek has been hosting Slug Fest for 25 years (take that, Elma!) for one weekend each June. They used to hold slug races, too, but they stopped because, well, it got boring. It can take a slug more than nine hours to finish a 100-yard "dash." Instead, they have a race for humans in slug costumes. The park also displays an impressive array of slugs, including Washington's native banana slug, a spotted green, yellow and brown specimen that looks like a banana and is often the length of one. Banana slugs are the second-largest slugs in the world, and Slug Fest pays tribute to this "beautiful" (their words, not ours) misunderstood mollusk.

Slug Fest offers all kinds of slime-filled fun. Visitors can earn a diploma in Slugology in "Slug School," play Slug Bingo, go on a slug hunt, play with pseudo slug slime, enjoy a game of slug toss (no actual slugs are harmed in the process of this game), nibble slug slime treats and "sluggle up" for a slime-time story. There's also a nature trail exploration, menu planning on what slugs like to eat and classes with master gardeners for adults and children on how to keep slugs from eating your whole garden. There's even a Slug Scavenger Hunt. No, you don't have to collect slugs; you just track down clues and slug facts throughout the park. At Slug Fest, those slimy slugs don't seem so bad, after all.

COMBINE DEMOLITION DERBY
LIND

Small town U.S.A. can't be better represented than it is in Lind. The modest wheat farming community, tucked away in the southeastern portion of the state in Adams County, has only 582 residents, but 5000 visitors from all over the United States flood the town each June. The reason? Lind has the oldest and largest (and only annual) Combine Demolition Derby in America. When the local Lions Club added the event to punch up Lind's Centennial Celebration in 1988, they thought maybe it would bring in a little revenue and get a few more locals to attend. They had no idea what they had started. The three-day Demolition Derby is now one of the region's most popular events, offering, as their posters pronounce, "a crushin' good time."

First, contestants rescue an old, nonworking combine from the junkyard. Wheat threshers must be at least 25 years old and completely useless in the field. Next, the teams modify the combines—fix them up so they work again and garishly redecorate them—and then bring them to the derby, where they inevitably get trashed again. It's the ultimate thrill for overgrown boys (and a few girls) who love to smash stuff up. There's also an inoperable combine beauty contest for the ones that just won't run.

At the 20th annual derby in 2007, 15 combines representing 12 different towns smashed and crashed at speeds of up to 15 miles per hour. The derby consists of several 15-minute heats in the dirt, then allows 30 minutes for repairs before the final heat. Of course, the goal in the arena is to disable your opponents' vehicles. The official rules mandate that drivers must be aggressive. They have only three minutes to make contact with another combine, or they're out. The result is mayhem. Machines weighing 10,000 pounds aim for each other's rear axles. Metal scrapes metal. Combines smash into one another with a force that outdoes any car crash, and then come back for more. The crunch is deafening. Finally, the huge pieces of farming equipment are demolished to the point where they no longer move and must be dragged out of the arena. The last one standing is the winner.

Cash prizes are awarded to the winner of each heat, and the lone survivor is named champion. In 2007, there were two survivors, each awarded a hefty $1750. But it's more about the rush than the money. Contestants return year after year because they say there's nothing else quite like it. The Combine Demolition Derby has recently added a Grain Truck Race to be held during intermission. There's no telling what they'll come up with next. The Derby has been featured on Country Music Television, and—believe it or not—earned a spot in *Playboy*'s 50th Anniversary Special Edition.

BIG
GARGANTUAN & RIDICULOUSLY OVERSIZED

HAT 'N' BOOTS
Georgetown

Never fear, fans of roadside attractions! The beloved, gargantuan Hat 'n' Boots sculpture is not gone! It's just been moved. Once the site of the Hat 'n' Boots Service Station, the stylish shell of a business gone defunct was rescued by the parks team and carted from 6800 Corson Avenue South in Oxbow Park, Georgetown, to 6400, just down the street. Georgetown is south of Seattle, and this adorable oddity has brightened up the drive south since 1955. It was built as part of the Premium Tex gas station. The 44-foot-wide hat topped off the office, and the 22-feet-high boots served as funky his and her restrooms. Straight out of the gate, the Hat 'n' Boots helped the station sell more gas than any other gas station in the state. But progress interfered. I-5 opened, and vehicles went that-away instead of on the old Pacific Highway (Route 99) where the Hat 'n' Boots were waiting to fill 'er up. The legendary station started to draw more visitors than customers. It was featured in the opening credits of *National Lampoon's Vacation* but didn't have enough real business to survive, and it closed down in 1988.

For 15 years it sat on the empty lot, a relic of the good ole days of Americana. The Department of Natural Resources owned the land and wanted the structure moved. In 2003, the Hat 'n' Boots was escorted down the street, one piece at a time, with the good people of the Parks Teamare slowly, lovingly restoring it as funding becomes available. Scuffed or not, the Boots ('n' Hat) will hang around for years to come.

OMAK STAMPEDE AND WORLD FAMOUS SUICIDE RACE
OMAK

Omak is home to the controversial World Famous Suicide Race, where riders, mostly Native Americans from the Colville Indian Reservation across the water, race their horses down a nearly vertical 210-foot fall above and then through the icy Okanogan River. This dangerous descent down "Suicide Hill" has resulted in the death of 20 horses since 1983 and countless broken human bones, all in pursuit of a $15,000 prize. Three horses perished in 2004 alone.

The Suicide Race started in 1935 as a publicity stunt for the annual Omak Stampede, a professional rodeo and Wild West show. Today, the centerpiece of the stampede is the race itself, which has been billed "the World's Most Dangerous Horse Race." About 20 riders compete each year, hurling themselves down the 30-degree hill at breakneck speed. Even if they survive Suicide Hill, they're not done yet. Next comes a too-narrow opening at the river's edge where the horses knock each other over to squeeze through. They tear into the rocky Okanogan River for a panicked swim across and then scramble uphill in a rush toward the finish line. The race isn't easy on the riders, either. They routinely break bones, and some have been thrown on their heads. But they have a choice in the matter, and they're the ones who get the money at the end.

Obviously, this extreme form of horse racing has drawn criticism from animal rights groups and the media. Defenders of the race say it preserves cultural tradition. It's true that the Suicide Race was once a Native American tradition, but this is the only one in America that still runs. Despite a boycott and cancellation of the race in 1999, and continuing critical press, the Omak Stampede's Suicide Race carries on, attracting a crowd of 8000 people per year.

SAW 'N' SURF CHAINSAW CARVING COMPETITION
WESTPORT

Call it cutting-edge art. The Westport Saw 'n' Surf Invitational Chainsaw Carving Competition held each September features 35 of the most talented professional carvers from the U.S. and Canada. The three-day event transforms the Westport Marina into one big workshop, with dust flying everywhere, and sponsors give ear plugs to the 2000 spectators. A local radio station emcees the show and broadcasts live with the buzzing in the background. The carvers vie for the distinction of best among the best as they saw away at enormous slabs of cedar and spruce. The catch? Their creations must be nautical in theme, hence the title Saw 'n' Surf. The grand-prize winner gets a cash prize and a brand new Echo CS-345 chainsaw. The audience gets to bid on the carvings, which range in price from $40 to $4000.

Artists also compete in "quick carve" contests daily, which give them just over an hour to complete a carving. The winning sculpture is the one that brings in the most money at auction. They have 15.5 hours over the course of the three days to complete their main piece, which is judged by a panel. The main piece is the artist's to keep. The carving process is just as entertaining to observe as the final creations, with the carvers performing for the crowd while wielding their chainsaws. At the end of the competition, the weekend's work is displayed up and down Westhaven Drive so that visitors can compare the chainsaw sculptures and vote for their favorites. The result is the buzz-worthy "People's Choice Award."

HOT AIR BALLOON STAMPEDE
WALLA WALLA

The Hot Air Balloon Stampede has brightened the sky at Walla Walla County Fairgrounds for 34 years. The Pacific Northwest's first and most prestigious hot air balloon rally attracts 40 of the region's finest pilots each May for a three-day celebration.

Balloons launch at sunrise each morning of the festival, but some families arrive even earlier to watch as they are inflated. Forty beautiful balloons suddenly fill the sky with color, launching from a single field over the course of an hour. Some folks jump in their vehicles to follow the balloons' trails, hoping to catch a glimpse of one as it lands. On Saturday evening, the Nite Glow Show illuminates the air. At dusk, all the hot air balloons

are blown up to a standing position throughout the enormous fairground and released into the sky like glowing balls of fire. An outdoor grandstand concert follows, complete with fireworks. Your neck will hurt from staring up above, but it will be worth it.

The family-friendly festival offers plenty of things to do when you're not balloon-watching, including a Friday night outdoor dance party, a champagne reception with air balloon pilots, a classic car show, horse racing, a juried art show, an arts and crafts fair, live music and a play zone just for children. But it's those bright balloons sailing through the sky that will make you get a little carried away.

BIG
GARGANTUAN &
RIDICULOUSLY
OVERSIZED

DINOSAUR PARK
Granger

Down in Granger, the sculptures don't depict the area's human history and aren't at all abstract. They do, however, highlight what Granger is famous for—the discovery of woolly mammoth bones in 1958. Although the bones were discovered in an abandoned clay mine, and the mining industry that served as the economic backbone for the community was in decline, the citizens came up with an idea that would keep their small town in the public eye. They branded their community with the motto, "Where Dinosaurs Roam," and in 1994 Granger began building and erecting life-sized dinosaurs throughout the community. The wire-mesh-covered steel frames are coated in concrete and painted with automotive paint. The first dinosaur completed was a brontosaurus, followed by a tyrannosaurus rex and a triceratops. Today, there are at least 12 dinosaur scenes scattered throughout the town and in Dinosaur Park, and if you have to go to the loo, you'll find yourself seated on a replica of a volcano.

DAFFODIL BED RACE
PUYALLUP

The giant, corporate-sponsored 17-day Puyallup Fair may be the town's famous one, but the most interesting festival in Puyallup is the "Daffodil 200" Bed Race held in August. It's also one of the most unique fundraisers. The bed race raises money for the Puyallup Community Float, which travels to more than a dozen festivals throughout the West, including the San Diego Holiday Bowl Parade. Participants must have a float to take part in Puyallup's Daffodil Festival.

Since 1985, the community has divided into teams and pushed wrought-iron beds around South Hill Mall every summer in a 200-yard dash toward the finish line. The winners get a trophy; the slowest team receives the Slug Award; and the Community Float Committee receives all the money raised, to ensure that Puyallup is represented at festivals all over the West, bringing publicity and revenue back to the city. Sounds like a race in which everybody wins.

BOB'S JAVA JIVE
Tacoma

Bob's Java Jive on South Tacoma Way is shaped like a coffeepot—a 25-foot-tall coffeepot. It used to be called, believe it or not, the Coffee Pot Restaurant. It's the last surviving giant structure on a street that once boasted a gas-pump-shaped service station and a lemon-shaped restaurant named Lemon Lunch. Nothing like the obvious. Bob's Java still jives, but now it's more of a dive bar than a coffee shop or restaurant. Live music and karaoke liven up the place, which is percolating with kitsch value.

Bring Out Yer Dead

The Green River is a picturesque 65-mile-long river, but it's not known for its natural beauty. Instead, it's infamous as the place where a serial killer disposed of his first five victims. Washington has at least 25 other serial murderers, most of whom are serving time in the state prison.

In this section, you are invited to indulge your sense of the macabre and explore the darker side of Washington history. We'll follow some of these serial killers' tracks, revisit local massacres and pay our respects at famous gravesites. We'll spy on the psychiatric hospital where an actress was held against her will, the house where a singer took his own life and a bridge where hundreds of residents have tragically committed suicide. Then we'll let you recover with a stiff drink at a mortuary that's been turned into a bar. Fasten your seat belts, it's gonna be a bumpy ride.

WASHINGTON STATE: SERIAL KILLER HAUNTS AND HOMES

HOME OF GARY LEON RIDGEWAY
AUBURN

Washington's most famous serial killer, Gary Ridgeway, murdered at least 48 women, all within King County. He is known as the "Green River Killer" because the bodies of his first five victims were found in the river itself or on its bank. Ridgeway himself led police to burial sites of other remains, including a now-infamous dig site near Kent-Des Moines Road.

For 32 years, Ridgeway was a model employee at Kenworth Truck Company on North 8th Street in Renton. Kenworth is a subsidiary of Bellevue-based Paccar, the third most successful truck maker in the world. Ridgeway worked there as a painter. As he was leaving work on November 30, 2001, he was arrested for seven murders. The paint he used at work linked him to three of the victims; the rest were linked by the landmark use of DNA.

The Green River Killer last lived in Auburn on a private, dead-end road with his family, who claimed to know nothing of his double life. The house lies near Military Road in a normal-looking middle-class community. Ridgeway now resides at the Washington State Penitentiary in Walla Walla.

HOME OF TED BUNDY
TACOMA

Ted Bundy is another serial killer with deep Washington roots. He grew up in a modest, unassuming house in Sky Line Drive in north Tacoma, where he was an active member of the First Methodist Church, a Boy Scout, a paper boy and a good student at Woodrow Wilson High School. Young Ted Bundy was awarded a scholarship to the University of Puget Sound (UPS), a private liberal arts college in the North End neighborhood of Tacoma on North Warner Street. Rumor has it that Bundy actually killed his first victim at UPS, dumping her body in the cement foundation of McIntyre Hall on campus, which was under construction at the time. But his earliest proven murders were committed in 1974 at the University of Washington in Seattle, where he'd graduated with a degree in psychology.

Bundy then moved on to Evergreen State College in the state capitol of Olympia, where he kidnapped and murdered another woman. Returning north to Ellensburg, he abducted a female student from the campus of Central Washington State College, now known as Central Washington University. His first non-student victim was taken from the parking lot outside the Flame Tavern, a joint with live music in working-class Burien, near Seattle-Tacoma International Airport. Bundy grew bolder as the year went on. His Washington murder spree culminated in two abductions in broad daylight at Lake Sammamish State Park, a scenic picnicking spot in the affluent bedroom community of Issaquah, about 12 miles east of Seattle. His victims' remains were found off of Interstate 90, just a few miles from the park.

Bundy confessed to killing at least 50 women, though the actual number may be as high as 100. Seattle's Private Eye Tours offers a sightseeing excursion through Seattle's underbelly that includes a drive by Bundy's old University District apartment and his nondescript gray dorm building on the University of Washington campus. The tour guide says Bundy kept the heads of some of his victims in that room. Yikes. A graveyard of some of his victims' skulls was found on the hillside of Taylor Mountain, just east of Issaquah. Beautiful, lush Taylor Mountain Forest encompasses 1840 acres that are popular for hiking, horseback riding and mountain biking, but Bundy had other plans for the secluded forest. It's difficult to imagine such atrocity amid a site of such natural beauty, home to deer, cougars, families of bears and the occasional elk.

Before his execution in Florida in 1989, Ted Bundy wrote to authorities from death row, offering to help them catch the Green River Killer. He bragged that he knew how a serial killer's mind worked. Indeed.

HOME OF ROBERT LEE YATES JR.
SPOKANE

And then there's Robert Yates, "the Spokane Serial Killer." He grew up in a middle-class household on scenic Whidbey Island, graduating from Oak Harbor High School. He attended Walla Walla College for two years before dropping out. Like Ridgeway, Yates targeted prostitutes as his victims, and like Bundy, he indulged in necrophilia. He was convicted of murdering 15 women, but he may have killed as many as 18. He took lives in at least four different counties in Washington: Spokane, Skagit, Pierce and Walla Walla, but his main trolling ground was Spokane's "Skid Row" red-light district (also known as Trent Alley) on East Sprague Avenue. Yates killed 13 prostitutes between 1996 and 1998, all lured from this street into his Ford van for sex.

In a bizarre twist, Yates dumped the bodies of five of his victims within 1.5 miles of his own home in the tiny, upper middle-class neighborhood of South Hill in Spokane. He also led police to the flower bed under his bedroom window, which was where he had buried one of his victims. The body was hidden just

8 inches below the surface, one foot from the foundation of the family home, for two years.

Ironically, Robert Yates once worked as a prison guard at the State Penitentiary in Walla Walla, the same place where he now serves his 408-year sentence. The penitentiary itself is a curiosity, located in a town otherwise populated by wine enthusiasts and tourists who flock to the region for three major wine tastings per year. There's a Holiday Inn Express across the street from the penitentiary, where the gift shop sells cheesy State Penitentiary T-shirts. And what a view the guests get.

But Wait, There's More...

Is it something in the water? Washington has had at least 25 recorded serial killers in addition to the big three. Two serial murderers have been executed at the Washington State Penitentiary in Walla Walla. One was serial child molester Westley Allan Dodd, a shipping clerk from Clark County who admitted to violating at least 30 children and murdering three boys in Vancouver, Washington. Dodd was caught after trying to abduct another young victim from a movie theatre in the small paper mill city of Camas in southeastern Washington. He was executed in 1993 in the first legal hanging execution since 1965.

James Elledge, who lived in a mobile home in Everett, followed. Elledge was convicted of sexual assault and two violent murders, including the murder of a female acquaintance in the bible study room in the basement of the Lighthouse Church in Lynnwood, where he worked as a custodian. Elledge was executed in 2001 by lethal injection.

Washington's nefarious offenders also include the "Want-Ad Killer" Harvy Carignan of Seattle (formerly a security alarm installation specialist in Bellingham), the "Eastside Serial Killer" George Russell of Mercer Island and the "Hillside Strangler" Kenneth Bianchi. Carignan left 18 bodies in his wake; Russell posed his victims post-mortem; and Bianchi, known for seven Los Angeles hillside murders, killed two Western Washington University Students in Bellingham in 1979. The roster of multiple murderers continues with Seattle native and army sergeant Dwayne Elton; Renton trailer park Navy enlistee Gary Grant and Spokane produce salesman Stanley Bernson, suspected of killing 30 Northwest women but convicted of only two. Bernson stabbed a 15-year-old girl to death and left her in a shallow makeshift grave in Richland (most famously known as the home of the Manhattan Project). Among the most grisly and scarring to the local psyche is sexual psychopath James Edward Ruzicka, an escapee of Western State Hospital for the Insane at Steilacoom, about 35 miles south of Seattle. Upon his escape, Ruzicka terrorized the neighborhood of West Seattle, hanging the body of one of his teenage rape victims from a tree. All of these men are prison, most here in Washington State.

WHITMAN MASSACRE
WALLA WALLA COUNTY

In southeastern Washington, 6 miles west of Walla Walla, lies the Whitman Mission National Historic Site and Whitman Massacre Site Interpretive Center. The Whitman Massacre, sometimes referred to as the Whitman "Incident" or the Walla Walla Massacre, marked the murders of 14 settlers from the Waiilatpu Mission in November 1847 by Native Americans of the Cayuse and Umatilla tribes. The 14 bodies were buried together in a single "Great Grave" at the bottom of what is now Whitman Monument hill, named for the Christian missionaries Dr. Marcus Whitman and his wife, Narcissa, who were among the dead. The massacre sparked the Cayuse War and is referenced as one of the most notorious chapters of U.S. settlement of the Northwest. In the pioneer days when the massacre occurred, the Waiilatpu Mission lay in what was then called "Oregon Country," which today is in southeastern Washington.

The pastoral memorial to the Whitmans makes little mention of grisly remains, instead spinning the massacre site as "a place to reflect upon the past, the future and ourselves" in a plea for tolerance. It offers visitors a balanced and carefully worded history lesson attributing the massacre to culture clash and an epidemic of measles. The influx of white settlers and their attempts to "save" Native American souls with the gospel were not exactly welcome. The Cayuse tradition involved gifts, which the settlers frowned upon as extortion. Cayuse spiritual and domestic practices took place concurrently, which the missionaries saw as sacrilege. The last straw was an epidemic of measles in 1847. Both the Cayuse and white settlers fell ill, and Dr. Whitman treated them all, but most of the whites and their children survived the sickness, while nearly half the Cayuse population, including almost all of their offspring, died. The Cayuse perceived this as treachery and burned down the mission, which resulted in war and the near destruction of the tribe.

The Cayuse War ended in 1855, but a series of fresh battles over the land ensued over the following 40 years and some unrest remains. The political history blankets the otherwise bucolic scene here with uneasiness, and the site's deceptive tranquility will keep your mind's wheels spinning long after your vehicle has pulled away.

WAH MEE MASSACRE
SEATTLE

Fast-forward to 1983 in Seattle's International District, formerly referred to as Chinatown. The Wah Mee club ("wah mee" loosely translates from the Chinese as "beautiful China") was a speakeasy gaming club that had been operating in a basement on Maynard Alley South since the 1920s. It was considered a classy joint, frequented by the wealthier clientele of the Chinese community, and the club housed one of the highest-stake gambling games around. That's exactly why it was targeted. Chinese immigrant Kwan Fai "Willie" Mak, 22, was drowning in his own gambling debts. He enlisted Wai-Chiu "Tony" Ng and Benjamin Ng (no relation) to help him rob the club. Just before midnight on February 18, the three stormed the Wah Mee club, shooting and killing 13 people. Just hours after their killing spree, Willie Mak and Benjamin Ng were captured. Tony Ng went into hiding in Canada but was caught two years later. All three men remain in prison. The club closed after the murders and remains padlocked (and sadly, defaced by graffiti). The once-opulent glass façade is layered with soot and grime, and the building itself is crumbling. But the story of what happened here endures, and locals still mourn at the scene of the crime.

CAPITOL HILL MASSACRE
SEATTLE

More recently, the Capitol Hill Massacre shattered the young rave community in Seattle in the city's largest mass murder since Wah Mee. In the early morning of March 25, 2006, 28-year-old Montana native Kyle Aaron Huff opened fire at a house party at 2112 East Republican Street, a peaceful, sprawling, blue two-story home in alternative Capitol Hill, killing six people, ages 14 to 32, before stepping out onto the porch to turn his 12-gauge shotgun on himself. Two others, both teenagers, were injured. The murderer had lived with his identical twin brother at Town and Country Apartments on Roosevelt Way Northeast in the industrial north Seattle neighborhood of Northgate, where they were referred to as the Teddy Bear Twins. Huff had scored an invite to the house party following a zombie-themed rave at the nearby Capitol Hill Arts Center called "Better Off Undead."

The blue house on East Republican was known as a haven among ravers and street kids—a non-judgmental place to be yourself, piercings, tats, purple hair and all. Rules were lax, but it was known as a safe place that reached out to loners, much like the residents were trying to do when they invited Huff because he looked lonely and out of place at the Capitol Hill Arts Center.

The shooting lasted less than four minutes but changed the landscape of this welcoming, carefree community forever. Some of the people who were there that night later removed the gunshot door from the bathroom in the house and took it with them to the Burning Man Festival in Nevada, where it illuminated the sky in a cathartic, ritualistic burn.

Life goes on at the house where seven young people died. The blue house has been painted green, scrubbed free of its painful history, and is now occupied by new tenants. Neighbors no longer like to talk about what happened. But we will always remember.

NOTABLE GRAVESITES, MEMORIALS AND THE MACABRE

BRUCE LEE'S GRAVE
SEATTLE

Internationally acclaimed martial artist and film director/actor Bruce Lee is revered as a cultural icon. Lee founded the Jeet Kune Do martial arts movement and made traditional Hong Kong martial arts films popular in America and all over the world. Though born in San Francisco, Lee moved to Seattle during high school and graduated from Edison Technical School. His third dojo was at 4750 University Way. Lee later attended the University of Washington, where he did not complete his studies but did meet his future wife, Linda Emery. They married in 1964. Less than 10 years later, with two small children, Lee, whose superhuman strength and agility were legendary, succumbed to acute cerebral edema and died at the age of 32. He was laid to rest at plot 276 of Lakeview Cemetery in Capitol Hill near Volunteer Park.

BRANDON LEE'S GRAVE
SEATTLE

In another tragedy for the family, Bruce Lee's son Brandon, an actor like his father, died at age 28 in a gun accident during the filming of the 1993 film *The Crow,* based on the comic book of the same name. Brandon died just weeks before he was to be married to fiancée Eliza Hutton. He is buried beside his father in Lakeview Cemetery. A memorial bench near the graves reads: "The key to immortality is first living a life worth remembering" and "Husband and Father, Son and Brother, You Are Always with Us—Linda and Shannon."

KURT COBAIN'S HOUSE
AND MEMORIAL BENCH
SEATTLE

One of Washington's most beloved music icons was Kurt Cobain, lead singer and guitarist for the grunge band Nirvana. The band played at the legendary (and now, defunct) Crocodile Café club in Seattle. If our Emerald City is known as the birthplace of grunge, it's largely because of Cobain (and his fellow rockers in Pearl Jam). Cobain was born in Hoquiam, Washington, and lived with Hole lead singer Courtney Love and their daughter

Frances Bean at 171 Lake Washington Boulevard East. On April 8, 1994, at only 27 years old, Cobain was found dead in the greenhouse above the home's garage after shooting himself. Courtney Love demolished the greenhouse after his suicide. Linda's Bar and Tavern, a popular dive on East Pine Street in Capitol Hill, is supposedly the last place Cobain was seen alive.

Lakeview Cemetery denied Cobain a plot, citing the stampede of tourists at the gravesites of Bruce and Brandon Lee as an excuse. Instead, a memorial bench in his honor was placed in Viretta Park on the corner of 39th Avenue and East John Street, not far from his home. About a third of his ashes were scattered in the Wishkah River in Washington. Nirvana's last live album, titled "From the Muddy Banks of the Wishkah," refers to this river, where Cobain said he lived under a bridge after dropping out of high school.

JIMI HENDRIX'S GRAVE
RENTON

One of the greatest and most vibrant masters of the electric guitar, Jimi Hendrix was a Seattle native known for his flamboyant style and smashed guitars. The Experience Music Project pays tribute to his legacy, and he has his own memorial sculpture on Broadway on Capitol Hill. But Hendrix had a drug habit that led to a barbiturate overdose on September 18, 1970. He was found dead at the Samarkand Hotel in London, having asphyxiated on his own vomit (drugs are so glamorous). His body was brought back to Seattle and interred at Greenwood Memorial Park Cemetery in Renton. He lies under a memorial dome of granite with his autograph inscribed on each pillar. Above the grave is a pedestal featuring his famous Fender Stratocaster guitar. Family members and about 4000 fans visit his grave each year.

ROSLYN CEMETERY
ROSLYN

Roslyn, Washington, is famous for its alter-ego, Cicely, Alaska, on the popular 1990s television show, *Northern Exposure*. But Roslyn also has a bizarre historic cemetery that is segregated by fraternal organization, country of origin, and even religion. There are about 24 different sections, divided as follows: Serbian, Polish, Lithuanian, Red Men Lodge, Eagles, Veterans, Elks, Masonic Lodge, Old Knights of Pythia, New Knights of Pithia, and Old City, for starters. There's even a section for Druids, but apparently they're referring to the pre-Christian Celtic religious society, not a tree sorcerer or the kind of magical priest you'd find playing Dungeons & Dragons.

There are around 5000 graves, which comes as a surprise since Roslyn only has a population of about 850 people. But that's today. In its mining town heyday, the town boasted as many as 6000 residents. Mining accidents took their toll. Forty-five men were killed in the mines in 1892, and another cave-in took 10 lives in 1909. Eventually the mining industry itself died, leaving behind a ghost town. The cemetery remains as the greatest memorial of the settlers from all over the world who lived and worked in Roslyn.

SUICIDE BRIDGE
SEATTLE

Aurora Bridge is a historic landmark. It's also the second-deadliest suicide bridge in the United States. "Suicide Bridge," as it is known to locals, is 155 feet high, as tall as a 15-story building. More than 230 people have jumped to their deaths from the bridge, 50 of them in the last decade, and nine in 2006 alone—the highest number in a single year, tying with 1972 as the worst

year yet. The first suicide occurred before the bridge even opened. The half-mile structure was built in 1931, and in 1932, a month before it opened to the public, a shoe salesman jumped off.

Scientists estimate that the free fall lasts less than four seconds, and a body will have reached about 55 miles per hour by the time it makes impact. Only one person has survived this fall. Some jumpers fall into the water, while others land on pavement, sometimes in the parking lot. Nearby workers are understandably traumatized. One body fell from the sky onto a moving SUV (the driver was shocked, but not hurt). One of the jumpers was a former SeaTac City Council member.

To address the problem, the Seattle government installed six emergency phones and 18 enormous signs broadcasting the number of a 24-hour crisis line. And in December 2007, Governor Chris Gregoire went a step further, dedicating $1.4 million to building an 8-foot suicide-prevention fence on the bridge, in the hopes that it can be plain old Aurora Bridge again.

FRANCES FARMER'S HOSPITAL OF HORRORS
STELLACOOM

Broadway and film actress Frances Farmer was born in Seattle in 1913. Her spirited, outspoken personality earned her the nickname "bad girl of West Seattle" at West Seattle High. She attended the University of Washington and is rumored to have lived at 312 Harvard Avenue East during her youth. Yet her traumatic adulthood post-stardom is what made her most famous. Farmer was forcefully institutionalized for six years at what was then Western State Hospital for the Insane, at Steilacoom (yes, the same one from which murderer James Ruzicka had escaped). Her own mother filed a complaint in King County Court asking that Farmer be declared legally insane. Farmer's court-appointed attorney waived her right to a jury trial, and Farmer was declared insane on the basis of agitation, delusions and paranoia. In a sign of the times, they also testified that "marital difficulty" may have contributed to the diagnosis.

Farmer was committed to the hospital in 1944 and released three months later, pronounced cured. Her case was used as an example of the success of electroshock therapy. But by the next year, after a California arrest for vagrancy, she was sent back, this time for five years. Western State Hospital in the mid-1940s has been described as a house of horrors—2700 patients were attended by only 15 graduate nurses. A fire in one decrepit building killed two patients in 1947. Farmer was subjected again to electroconvulsive shock therapy, resulting in memory loss. After her release, she tried to resurrect her career but could not remember her lines. Instead she got a job at the Olympic Hotel in Seattle where, in 1936, she had been a source of hometown pride at the world premiere of her film, *Come and Get It*. Now she was sorting laundry. Farmer died, destitute, of esophageal cancer in 1970 at the age of 56. She was buried in Indianapolis, but her rebellious spirit lives on in Seattle, with the help of two other locals—Washington native Jessica Lange, who portrayed Frances Farmer in the 1982 film *Frances*, and Kurt Cobain, who wrote a song about her called "Frances Farmer Will Have Her Revenge on Seattle," on the album *In Utero*.

CHAPEL BAR
SEATTLE

Chapel Bar on Melrose Avenue in Capitol Hill was originally built in the 1920s as a chapel inside the Butterworth Mortuary. A photograph of Bruce Lee's funeral procession shows his casket being carried out of the mortuary's Pine Street entrance. The former funeral home chapel retains some of its original architecture—stained glass windows, enormous pillars, formidable wooden doors, a vaulted roof and a long marble staircase. The entrance bears a basin for holy water, but it's now filled with matchbooks. Everything at "Chapel," as they call it, is dark. The wood, the lighting, the surly nature of the bartender…but the bar itself is a stunning centerpiece of ghostly white. Perilously high white stools circle a smooth, cold, stone structure with small numbered markers for the urns that used to be there. Rumor has it that the structure is an authentic piece from the mortuary basement. It feels like mausoleum marble, all right.

Gothic wrought-iron candelabras add to the ambiance. Chapel certainly gets you in the mood for spirits—the drinkable kind and the ones they say haunt the place after closing time.

DIRTY BITER MEMORIAL
LA CONNER

You can visit an odd little monument to a mangy-looking mutt and, in the process, learn a bit of La Conner's weird folklore. The story goes that a pup, which based on its reincarnation in bronze looked to be at least part pit-bull, came along in the early 1970s and captured everyone's heart in La Conner. No one really knew where he'd come from or to whom he belonged. The mutt just hung around near his favorite tavern, which at the time went by the name of 1890s Tavern, and pretty much endeared himself to anyone who cared to donate a show of affection or, if you were a really nice kind of dog lover, a morsel of food. Dirty Biter, as the dog came to be known, was pretty much owned by the entire town, though he quite likely didn't live up to his name, or he may have found himself bunking in the neighborhood pound.

In any case, the tavern owners made sure Dirty Biter was fed and watered, and he continued to live this way until 1982 when he was out-muscled and died in a dogfight. Folks were so devastated by his tragic death that they organized a life-sized monument be created in his memory. The Dirty Biter Memorial can be seen at none other than Dirty Biter Park on First Street. A nearby sign recounts Dirty Biter's story and ends with the endearment, "Dirty Biter—Our Hero."

PICKLED PIONEER
MENLO

We all know drinking and driving is a definite no-no, but this is one time when someone wouldn't have arrived at all had he not been pickled—but not in the way you're thinking. The story goes back to May 1855, when Dr. William Keil led a group of colonists to Washington from Bethel, Missouri. He'd promised his son, 19-year-old Willie Jr., that he'd be responsible for leading the way, except that young Willie came down with malaria and died just four days before the group were supposed to leave. So to keep his promise, and keep his family together, the good doctor placed his son in a lead-lined coffin, filled it with the best, most powerful alcohol around, and ordered that it lead the group.

The doctor and his entourage safely made it to their destination, near Menlo, and young Willie was finally laid to rest on December 26, 1855. A memorial plaque outlining the story marks the young Willie's resting place along what is now a lonely stretch of State Route 6. Curiously, Tombstone Willie's Saloon is located directly across the road.

Oddball Towns

Washington takes pride in being weird. Leading the pack of the state's most peculiar places is Fremont, the self-proclaimed "Center of the Universe." Washington's cosmos also includes its own Troll Village, Bavarian Disneyland, Little Norway and Wild West. Bet you didn't know that Cicely, Alaska, is in Roslyn, Washington, where they filmed Northern Exposure *for five years in the 1990s. You'll find the famous Twin Peaks here, too, in North Bend where the Double R Diner still serves up that famous cherry pie.*

DISTINCTIVE DESTINATIONS AND TOURIST TRAPS

FREMONT
SEATTLE

Welcome to Fremont, the self-proclaimed "Center of the Universe." This is the quirky little neighborhood known as Seattle's Left Bank, where naked bicyclists zoom past a Volkswagen-eating troll and a bronze statue of Vladimir Lenin on their way to a working rocket. And that's only the first few blocks. Eccentricity is a perfected art form here. In fact, the People's Republic of Fremont, as the community sometimes calls itself, once voted to secede from Seattle to assert its individuality and ensure its continuing creative freedom. Artist activists organized to declare Fremont an independent state—of mind. But they settled for an official proclamation from Metropolitan King County Council, stating:

> *Whereas, Fremont is a State of Mind, not a foreign nation but an ImagiNation based on the freedom to dream...Now, therefore, be it proclaimed by the Council of King County: The Artistic Republic of Fremont is hereby declared, decreed and determined to be an Independent ImagiNation and a Mecca for those of independent minds and spirits, and is forever and fervently empowered with all the rights and privileges thereto accruing. Further, the Metropolitan King County Council plainly postulates and proclaims Fremont to be Center of the Universe, indeed, and hereby supports Fremont in its gallant endeavors to apply to the United Nations for sovereign status under international law. Dated this twenty-fifth day of July, 1994.*

So, Fremont actually is the Center of the Universe, according to King County Council Chair Kent Pullen and Cynthia Sullivan of District Two. Blame them!

Present-day Fremont is sort of like New York's Greenwich Village was in the 1960s. Or Berkeley, California, anytime. Free-spirited Fremont's official motto is *De Libertas Quirkus*, which means "Freedom to be Peculiar." That freedom is exercised in the signature Fremont Solstice Parade each June.

The Painted Cyclists kick off the parade, covered in bright body paint and not much else. (Using sunscreen is important. Solstice Cyclist Rob got a plaid sunburn in 2002.) They burst into

downtown Fremont in a streak of color, perched atop equally irreverent, decorated "art bikes," rickshaws, unicycles, tandems and tricycles. No motor vehicles take part in this parade, just pure fossil fuel-free fun. There are also no live animals, no weapons, no logos and no written words allowed, but beyond that, there are no rules. The whimsical celebration takes its cue from Mardi Gras, with elaborate towering puppets, dragon heads, an undulating procession of 100 belly dancers, colorful floats and even more colorful street performers—the more outrageous, the better. (The return of the sun is a big deal when you live in Seattle.) Freaky Fremont kicks up its heels in a joyful explosion of creativity and community. The parade dances its way to Gas Works Park, where it culminates in the Solstice Pageant. There, neighborhood folks adorn themselves with elaborate masks and costumes to enact a theatrical presentation of a modern myth with a message. The party continues until sundown. The Fremont Arts Council produces the event, which started in 1989. They're the entity behind the surge of public art, and they extend an open invitation to all to stop by the sunburst-painted Powerhouse to build floats and build kinship.

Another fun and funky part of the two-day festival is The Art Car Blowout, the third-largest art car show in the nation. Seventy-five uniquely decked-out cars are on display, looking like canvasses on wheels. You can check out the Floppy Disc Car with "escape" computer keys on the doors, a leopard print "Zoobaru" with hand-painted spots and a feline face, and a fuzzy pink marabou concoction with bizarre Barbie heads marching along the hood. Raffle tickets for one of the cars (in 2007, it was the "Garden of Love") are sold to benefit Solid Ground, formerly the Fremont Public Association, which works to fight poverty and racism.

The Solstice Parade and Pageant is just one day in the life of Fremont. Public art is on tap here 24/7. It starts at the Fremont Drawbridge, where a neon Rapunzel is forever letting down her hair. Right after the bridge is the beloved aluminum sculpture "Waiting for the Interurban," which depicts a quiet crowd waiting in perpetuity for a light rail that no longer runs. But look closer and you'll see that the dog in the sculpture has a human face. Rumor has it that the artist, Richard Beyer, gave the dog the face of Arman Napoleon Stepanian, unofficial mayor of Fremont, because he refused to pay for the sculpture as promised. But the official Fremont website states that the mayor's "dogged" persistence got Seattle to partake in curbside recycling. I like the first story better. The sculpture is frequently subjected to spontaneous "art attacks." Locals routinely dress it up for holidays, football games, political demonstrations or even just for the hell of it. "Waiting for the Interurban" presents an accurate reading of Fremont's temperature at any given moment.

But the real star of Fremont is the troll lurking under the Aurora Bridge. The Fremont Troll is an 18-foot-tall concrete creature, clutching a real Volkswagen Beetle in his fist and staring you down with a single shiny silver hubcap eye. Steve Badanes

brought the gargantuan ogre to life in 1989 from 2 tons of ferro-concrete, wire and rebar steel.

Despite the troll's size and legendary car-eating reputation, he's more endearing than scary. Interaction is encouraged. Visitors climb his arms for photo ops and look up inside his nose. Locals bring him offerings and celebrate his birthday, October 31. Halloween is Troll-o-ween in these parts, with drum circles, performance art and an orange spotlight on the troll, who seems to enjoy all the attention.

If you head toward the taco place on North 36th Street, you'll bump into an unlikely suspect: a 7-ton bronze likeness of Russian revolutionary Vladimir Lenin. Washington resident Lewis Carpenter found the statue lying face-down in Slovakia when he was teaching there. It had been toppled during the 1989 revolution that dismantled the Soviet Union. Drawn to the statue's artistry, Carpenter mortgaged his house, bought the statue and brought it back home. When he died suddenly in 1994, his family loaned the statue to Fremont for public display. This Lenin is unlike any other, though. Slavic artist Emil Venkov portrayed him surrounded by flames and guns instead of the usual books. The statue's towering presence still causes controversy. Some worry that it makes light of the violent tactics employed by Lenin's regime. Others enjoy the irony of communist Lenin's location in front of the Taco Del Mar food chain. The Fremont Arts Commission points to the statue as proof that art outlives politics. Oh, and Lenin's for sale, in case you know someone who supposedly has everything.

Down the street from Lenin is the Fremont Rocket, erected in 1994. The 53-foot tall missile (declared the Republic of Fremont's armed forces) is a Korean-made Cold War artifact rescued from the junkyard. It used to belong to AJ's Surplus in the Belltown section of Seattle. Arts activists restored it, adding new fins, installing neon laser pods and decorating it with a galaxy mural. By the time the rocket made its debut in the Center of

the Universe, it bore the Fremont crest and official motto.
A coin-operated "launch mode" sends steam vapor rising from
its base, but fear not, this rocket's not going anywhere. Yet.

Fremont may need those armed forces, after all. Since 2004,
it's been plagued by zombies—150 of them invade the neighborhood each October, eager to feed on human brains. Fremont's
Zombie Walk hijacks the fair village with a lurching procession
of the undead. The usually carefree culture turns to terror as the
zombies' only responses to the various implements protruding
from their gray-blue heads are vacant, glassy stares. The horrific
hordes hunch their way through the organic market, inching
toward the living in the used bookstore. Like other marches in
Seattle, the Zombie Walk even has its own activist chant: "What
do we want?" "Brains!" "When do we want them?" "Now!"
Bloodcurdling screams turn to appreciative applause saluting
the effort. The creative costumes and elaborate make-up
approach a professional level. Indeed, among the zombie crowd
are actors, artists and film crews, as well as software engineers,
graphic designers, dog walkers and plain old fans of the genre—
and there's even a corpse bride in the flesh-eating flesh.

Just another day in Fremont, the Center of the Universe.

THE GROUCH
KETTLE FALLS

Sure, Kettle Falls is the home of 1992's Miss America, Carolyn
Suzanne Sapp, but its real claim to fame is the grouch. Drive
into this small northern town and a huge sign immediately
warns you of its population: "1550 friendly people and one
grouch." Before you worry about the unlucky person with that
title and wonder why he or she doesn't just move already, hear
this: it's an honor to be a grouch. The position is elected in a
kind of popularity contest each year. Residents nominate their

favorite curmudgeon and lobby for votes in an election that is most definitely bought. At 25 cents a vote, residents vote as often as they want—and ballot stuffing is actually encouraged! The political mayhem begins each April as a fundraising venture for the annual Kettle Falls Town & Country Days Celebration that takes place in June. The event includes a 4.5 mile Grumpy Grouch Fun Run, a parade down Main Street, logging events and an outdoor community church service. The amusement culminates in the eagerly anticipated announcement of the new Kettle Falls Grouch. There have been 22 grouches in the history of the town so far, and not one of them has been named Oscar.

BANDY'S TROLL HAVEN
GARDINER

The troll enjoys unprecedented popularity in Washington State. Never mind the giant troll lurking under the bridge in Fremont—the town of Gardiner, a ferry ride away on the Olympic Peninsula, is crawling with trolls! The imps populate Troll Haven, a 150-acre private estate/theme park built by Gary Bandy.

To visit Troll Haven is to journey into a mystical realm. Approach the imposing metal gate and a 15-foot Cyclops gives you the eye. If you look closely at the 100-yard fence, you'll see that each wooden post is hand-carved into a different troll. Each building in the park is painstakingly detailed with lavish sculptures and artwork of trolls, dragons and their magical friends. Eight-foot-high trolls hold up the barn from underneath, and a purple-robed troll guards the extravagant purple castle and Troll Museum. The castle's vast entryway leads to a circular staircase beneath an enormous crystal chandelier. Stained glass windows lend a gothic feel, as do hand-carved chairs dripping with ruby velvet. A labyrinthine dungeon lies beneath, lined with swords and various torture implements. Troll legend warns that these otherwise invincible creatures turn to stone when exposed to sunlight, which explains what must have happened to the granite gargoyles watching from the walls. Escape through the thick, iron-hinged oak doors to a lush, whimsical landscape on the glittering waterfront of Discovery Bay. Explore a topiary trimmed to resemble the Loch Ness monster. Play hide-and-seek with the mythical creatures peeking from the woods.

Bandy's vision lives everywhere—in the trees, in the woods, in the garden, immortalized in wood, stone and paint. Hand-carved trolls surprise you wherever your gaze lingers, each with its own distinctive personality. The barn houses a monstrous dragon, a fanged beast and a Nordic troll standing proud in a Viking helmet. There are mischievous trolls, cherubic trolls and trolls that are silly and decidedly wicked. There's a troll farm and a troll museum. A troll poem above the barn entrance sets the mood for this "refuge from the mundane, a place to dream and imagine." Just when you're getting used to all the imaginary creatures in this mystical sanctuary, you'll spot real buffalo and cattle through the window, roaming the grounds. There's also a Dragon's Keep area, but alas, no dragon.

Bandy originally intended for Troll Haven to serve as a tourist attraction, like a medieval Disneyland, but his neighbors in the tranquil town balked. It remains private property, but that doesn't mean you can't experience it firsthand. The castle can be rented for $2500 per month. There are even beds in the dungeon for Goth kids. You can also rent Troll Haven for a fairy tale wedding, Shrek style. And if you simply can't bear to leave this enchanting slice of paradise, it's currently for sale for $2.5 million.

BIG
GARGANTUAN &
RIDICULOUSLY
OVERSIZED

MILK BOTTLE BUILDINGS
Spokane

Believe it or not, I've actually been in a house designed in the shape of a shoe, as in the little old woman who lived in one. I also knew someone who built a stack wall house, which is a house basically built out of firewood logs. And I even know someone who lives a lot farther north than Spokane, and she lives in a house of straw. But this, my friends, is a first. Spokane was home to two buildings constructed in the shape of milk bottles. Built in 1935 as an advertising ploy, the Benewah Milk Bottle is currently listed on the National Register of Historic Places. The second such building, constructed by the same company, was last reported to be the home of a Garland Avenue burger joint. According to the spin doctors of the day, the milk bottle buildings were created to "build better men and women by making dairy products attractive to boys and girls."

LITTLE NORWAY
POULSBO

Poulsbo never strayed far from its roots. It's named for Paulsbo,
Norway, because the Norwegian settlers in the late 1800s
thought it looked like home, surrounded by snow-crowned
mountains and fjord-like Liberty Bay. Poulsbo's name is actually
a typo. When the village established its first post office, the
postmaster general couldn't read the handwriting and replaced
the "a" with an "o." No matter, the residents knew where they
were. They unpacked their heritage and made their new home
into what is affectionately called Little Norway.

Until World War II, Norwegian reigned as Poulsbo's official
language. Even now, a stroll through town surrounds you with
voices tinged with an unmistakable Scandinavian lilt.

Conversations are peppered with jargon such as "uff da" (to convey amazement) and "ja" instead of "yes." The scenery, too, is deliberately attuned to the town's heritage. Streets have names such as Viking Avenue and Fjord Drive Northeast. Scandinavian murals and façades adorn the many shops. The shops themselves are Scandinavian-themed, such as The Nordic Maid. Homesick Scandinavians and shop-happy tourists can find all manner of specialty treasures, from thick wool Norlender and Skjaeveland sweaters or traditional Swedish door harps to lefse grills and krumkake irons. Twelve miles away, most Seattleites know a lefse from a krumkake by osmosis, but for the rest of you, here's an explanation. Lefse is a native Norwegian recipe for a thin potato pancake that is served rolled up and is the size of a narrow finger. Krumkaker, traditionally made around Christmas, are sweet, round cakes baked on a decorative griddle and rolled into small cones.

Perhaps one of the best ways to immerse yourself in Norwegian culture is through their food. That's easy to do in Poulsbo. Legendary Sluys Bakery features the original, famous Poulsbo bread, made with sunflower seeds. This hearty bread is marketed nationwide and is commonly found in Washington grocery stores, but the real thing, straight from the source, somehow tastes even better. A traditional food that's not quite as easy to swallow is lutefisk, a Nordic dish of dried whitefish, usually cod, soaked in lye. The name literally means "lye fish." Lutefisk season in Poulsbo begins in October, when the First Lutheran Church holds its annual Lutefisk dinner. It's a recurring meal throughout Christmas.

Each May, visitors are treated to a Norwegian history lesson with Poulsbo's extraordinary Viking Fest. For 40 years, Poulsbo has hosted this lively celebration of Norwegian Constitution Day. Norwegians themselves call it simply "syttende mai," or the 17th of May. This is the day the Norwegian Constitution was signed in Eidsvoll in 1814, officially making Norway an independent country. This tribute to their forefathers is observed in Poulsbo as it is in Norway, with a children's promenade, flag festival, the Norwegian anthem and traditional costumes. The Poulsbo version goes a step further though, extending the celebration to three days and including a road race, music and entertainment at Kvelstad Pavilion, an all-you-can-eat pancake breakfast, a waterfront parade, an authentic Viking village, performances by folk dancers and the Kitsap County Cloggers, and fireworks.

Viking Fest arose organically out of the villagers' heritage, and everything about it feels authentic. Well, everything except the Americanized eating contest and Miss Viking Fest pageant. But while the next big empire is hatched in Starbucks' headquarters, and the latest technology is produced at Microsoft campus in Redmond, Poulsbo steadfastly maintains its Nordic traditions and protects its native culture.

THAT ONE-HORSE TOWN
ENUMCLAW

As long as we're talking about ogres, it's hardly a matter of civic pride, but a bizarre bestiality death brought the rural community of Enumclaw, Washington, to nationwide attention in 2005. The shocking story was widely distributed and passed around the Internet. The *Seattle Times'* articles about the subject, carefully non-sensationalized, are still among the most-read pieces in the newspaper's history. Like it or not, it's now part of ours.

In Enumclaw, the men are men, and the horses are scared. Or maybe the men should be scared, too, since it was the horse that survived in this mismatched couple. Forty-five-year-old Boeing employee Kenneth Pinyon became infamous after his death by copulation with an Arabian stallion. The County Medical Examiner ruled that Pinyon's demise resulted from a perforated colon. This sad and repugnant event shone a spotlight on

Washington state's surprising lack of a law against such behavior. At the time, it was not actually illegal to engage in bestiality in Washington. With the help of Pasado's Safe Haven (a nonprofit animal sanctuary in Sultan) and the Humane Society, the government corrected that omission in 2006 with a unanimously approved anti-bestiality bill. Bestiality is now against the law, as well as a crime against nature, and Washington joins the other 30 states that protect their animals from this kind of abuse.

The "Enumclaw horse sex death," as it's been called, uncovered a ring of local men engaging in this behavior at the same Enumclaw farm (the poor owners, who merely rented the property, had no idea what was going on behind closed barn doors). The fetishists apparently connected through chat rooms, illustrating the downside of the technology-obsessed Pacific Northwest. Pinyon's death also inspired Seattle filmmakers Robinson Devor and Charles Mudede to make a strange documentary about the local "zoophiliac community" (zoophilia refers to an "abnormal fondness for animals"). Titled *Zoo*, the film was bought by a New York distributor and debuted at Sundance and the Cannes Film Festival. With the advent of Netflix, we'll never live it down.

LITTLE BAVARIA
LEAVENWORTH

Vilkommen to Leavenworth! This fanciful Bavarian village in the Wenatchee Valley has only 2000 residents yet plays host to more than one million visitors each year. It's all part of their fairy tale history as the Little Town That Could.

Once upon a time, Leavenworth was a happy little logging town with its own sawmill. Then one day, the Great Northern Railway Company changed its route, leaving Leavenworth on the wrong side of the tracks. The mill closed, and the town's

economy took a nosedive. Streets that once bustled with business evaporated into a near ghost town. But the people of Leavenworth didn't give up. They put their heads together to come up with a solution. "Maybe," they thought, "maybe if we reinvent the town and give it a theme, people will come here to spend their money." They ran through a list of possibilities. "How 'bout the Gay '90s?" someone suggested. "Nah, not really interesting enough," was the general consensus. "How 'bout a Western town?" another piped up. "Washington already has two of those," said another. "What about an alpine village?" someone said. The room was silent. People began to get excited. "The Cascade Mountains do make a nice backdrop," somebody ventured. "We could make all the buildings look like Bavaria," another chimed in. "I know how to do that!" exclaimed one man. The people began to feel hopeful for the first time in years. "Let's see if we can get a loan from the bank." "Let's work together to save our town!" The group approached the towns-people and the local banks. Everyone pitched in to help. And so Leavenworth as we know it, that little Bavarian Disneyland in the middle of Washington, was born.

By the late 1960s, the idea had caught on. A bit of Bavaria pervades every building in town, even the Safeway supermarket and the local gas station. In fact, I dare you to find a building in downtown Leavenworth that doesn't adhere to the theme. In the square, a town crier announces local events such as Maifest, where men in lederhosen play their accordions as women in traditional Alpine dirndl dresses gather round the maypole. Couples dance the polka and wash bratwurst and alpenhorns down with German white beer.

Retail efforts encourage the tourist trade. No less than 145 Bavarian-themed shops dot the streets. A Nutcracker Museum displays a collection of 5000 nutcrackers dating back to the 1500s. It's Christmas all year round at a store called Kris Kringl. Since its second life as a fabricated Bavaria, Leavenworth has blossomed into a bona fide tourist trap, er, town. People come from all over to experience this slice of Germany at home. And the local cultural organization Projekt Bayern works to keep the tradition alive with new Bavarian-style offerings.

Among the most successful of these celebrations is Oktoberfest. Since the inaugural Leavenworth Oktoberfest in 1998, the event has attracted at least 1700 people and now lasts three consecutive weekends. In addition to genuine German beer, food, bands imported from Germany and dancing by the local troupe Edelweiss Tanz Gruppe, a Bier Wagon parades through the center of town. The mayor gets in on the act in a Keg Tapping Ceremony that re-enacts Bavarian custom. In recent years,

Leavenworth's Oktoberfest has been ranked as one of the top celebrations in the country.

Wintertime especially showcases this jewel box of a town. The Lighting Festival in December converts downtown Leavenworth into a wonderland before an audience of 25,000. White lights sparkle like stars in the snow, harkening back to a time when the town was known simply as "Icicle." Locals and tourists alike take in traditional annual performances of *The Sound of Music*. Santa arrives on Front Street in his sleigh, and families serenade him with Christmas carols. All is calm and bright in this little hamlet that brought itself back to life. And Washingtonians can get a dose of old Bavaria without even stepping on a plane.

WILD WEST
WINTHROP

The Wild West of Winthrop took a cue from Leavenworth's success. In 1972, Winthrop's timber trade was dying, bringing the town's economy down with it. The North Cascades Highway (also known as Washington State Highway 20) had recently been completed, and Winthrop's savvy citizens saw opportunity. The road would bring people through town; residents just had

to give them a reason to stop. They decided to perform their own makeover, transforming their town back into the old Wild West. The concept wasn't entirely out of left field. The townspeople capitalized on Winthrop's Methow Valley mining history and connections. Author Otis Wister, a Harvard classmate of the town's founder, Guy Waring, paid his college chum a visit in the late 1800s. He stayed in Winthrop, researching his famous western novel, *The Virginian*. Locals claim Wister based much of the book on Waring's story and Winthrop's humble beginnings.

The community of Winthrop acted quickly. They asked Leavenworth architects for help, and local patron Kathryn Wagner financed their efforts. The goal was to revive the town's mining and homesteading origins from 1885 and 1920. The short main drag of Riverside Avenue was painted over, Deadwood style. The log cabin Waring once lived in was preserved as a historical museum that locals call "the Castle." They lined the streets with wooden boardwalks, created decorative building façades and erected hitching posts. Add a cattle drive, a fiddle contest, a cowboy jamboree and old-fashioned Rodeo Days, and Winthrop's Wild West was born.

The formula added up to success. Truckloads of tourists passing through on their way to someplace else stopped to eat at Vittles Cowboy Café. They bought trinkets at White Buck Trading Company. They paused to admire Town Hall, originally the Duck Brand Saloon, which doubled as a church, hospital, school and pool hall in its day. The 400 townsfolk of Winthrop rebuilt their economy, welcoming 4000 visitors a year, and now their reconstituted frontier town is being called the next Jackson Hole, Wyoming. Washington has learned its lesson: when in doubt, try tourism!

THERE'S NO PLACE LIKE...
HOME

There's no place like Home. No, really. A town called Home
achieved notoriety in 1902. "Free love" started here well before
the '60s, when the free-spirited commune held shocking notions
for the 1880s, such as the idea that women should be allowed
to vote and religion should not be coerced. When the Mutual

Home Association was started by comrades from a Socialist colony east of Tacoma, they announced their intentions thusly: "One may, at Home, keep within the pale of the law or completely ignore it, just as he pleases." The libertarian community of peaceful anarchists made their Home 50 miles east of Mount Rainier and just north of Longbranch. Everyone lived as they pleased. Two men, Joe Kapolla and Franz Erkelems, even lived in a tree. The local paper disseminated its radical ideas. And that's where they got into trouble. The government closed Home's post office in 1902 because of its wanton circulation of progressive newspapers.

In the 1890s, a Tacoma jury accused Home denizens of indecent exposure for swimming nude. The town's editor, Jay Fox, published an editorial on "The Nudes and the Prudes" in the community paper, *The Agitator.* He was sent to jail in Tacoma for two months for "tending to encourage or advocate disrespect for law." The ruling was appealed all the way to United States Supreme Court, and upheld, though Fox was pardoned when Governor Lister took office. The editor's sentence was shortened by 12 days.

Home received regular visits by prominent anarchists such as Emma Goldman, but the relentless scrutiny took its toll. Utopia began to fray around the edges. The town store nearly went bankrupt, the meeting hall literally fell apart, and so did the colony. On September 10, 1919, the Mutual Home Association dissolved. Some of its nonconformists moved on, while others remained in what is now unincorporated Pierce County. The story of Home lives on as one of the more scintillating segments of state history and a precursor to modern-day liberal life in Seattle.

NORTHERN EXPOSURE'S CICELY
ROSLYN

Remember the Emmy Award–winning television series *Northern Exposure* from the 1990s? The one with the moose lumbering down the main street in its opening credits? That main street, supposedly in Cicely, Alaska (which doesn't exist), was actually right in Roslyn, Washington. Cicely's gift shop, a.k.a. Dr. Fleishman's office, remains, as does the Brick Tavern featured in so many of the show's episodes. Built in 1889, the tavern is the oldest, still-open saloon in the region. For proof, check under the bar, where you'll find a running water spittoon still in working order. Strolling through the town feels a little, no, scratch that, a *lot* like walking through a film set. There's the Roslyn Café and RuthAnne's General Store, and that must be the KBHR radio studio. Down this street you'll find Maggie's first house, and down another, her second.

For years, *Northern Exposure* fans trekked to Roslyn for its annual fan festival called Moosefest. Visitors were sometimes joined by stars of the show. Cynthia Geary, the actress who played young Shelly, still lives in Washington and makes occasional appearances in local films.

But there's more to Roslyn than *Northern Exposure.* Coal was said to be "discovered" here in 1882. Roslyn was home to the Northern Pacific Coal Mine, where a 25-ton hunk of the stuff was once touted as the biggest cut of its time. The industry attracted an unprecedented community of multi-ethnic workers, whose diversity is reflected in the town cemetery.

TWIN PEAKS
NORTH BEND

A television tour of Washington State would be incomplete without stopping by Twede's Café in North Bend. Formerly named Mar T Café, the famed eatery doubled as the Double R Diner in the 1991–92 cult hit television series and subsequent feature film, *Twin Peaks*. Constructed in 1942, the diner survived World War II, the Depression era, arson in 2000 and a robbery in which thieves made off with most of the *Twin Peaks* memorabilia. Home of "Twin Peaks Cherry Pie" and a "Damn fine cup of coffee," the diner is still a tourist attraction with photos and memorabilia displayed on its walls in a back corner. Sadly, these are all that remain of the collection. But fans can sit on the same stool where actor Kyle MacLachlan ate cherry pie as FBI Agent Dale Cooper, and the actual twin peaks of the show's title are visible outside the window. (Well, there's really only one peak.) Nearby, the stately exterior of the Salish Lodge & Spa in Snoqualmie, perched atop the majestic Snoqualmie Falls, served as the show's Great Northern Lodge.

BIG GARGANTUAN & RIDICULOUSLY OVERSIZED

LAURA'S LOG
North Bend

The Snoqualmie area is home to Laura's Log, the 39-ton log that was pictured at the start of every episode of ***Twin Peaks.*** "The Big Log," as it is known locally, rests at Snoqualmie's Historic Log Pavilion. In real life, it was donated by Weyerhaeuser Snoqualmie Falls Sawmill, which appeared in the show as Packard Sawmill. A local pharmacy still sells "Official Log Lady Logs" as firewood.

FRASIER'S CITY
SEATTLE

The hit television series *Frasier* won 37 Emmy Awards during its 11-year run from 1993 to 2004, breaking the previous record held by *The Mary Tyler Moore Show*. *Frasier* also immortalized Seattle's coffee culture with its fictional gourmet coffee shop, Café Nervosa. Although the show was set in Seattle, featuring a Space Needle view from Frasier Crane's apartment window, only one episode, the landmark 1000th show, was filmed in the city. The rest of the episodes were on the set of Paramount Studios' Studio 25. Sadly, there is no Café Nervosa in real life, though proud locals claim that the café was modeled after the Elliot Bay Café in the basement beneath the famed Elliot Bay Book Company on First Avenue and South Main Street. Café Nervosa was set on Third Avenue and Pine Street. Pop culture hounds get to see both stops on walking tours of the city.

It Happened Here: Washington Film History
Many movies were filmed in Washington, including *An Officer and a Gentleman, Sleepless in Seattle, Singles, Say Anything, War Games* and Elvis' *It Happened at the World's Fair*, but following the untimely death of 28-year-old actor Heath Ledger in 2008, locals have begun paying tribute to his breakout film, *10 Things I Hate About You*. The otherwise unremarkable 1999 romantic teen comedy was shot in Tacoma and Seattle, with scenes at the Fremont Troll, Gasworks Park, the Aurora Bridge, Century Ballroom, the Paramount Theater, Fremont Book Company, Ted Brown Music Company and Buckaroos Tavern. The home where Heath finally won Julia Stiles' character over is in the tiny Tacoma neighborhood of North End, and Tacoma's Stadium High School was used for exterior shots. These places gained new relevance after Ledger's passing, as local fans retraced the actor's footsteps in remembrance.

BLUEBIRD CAPITAL
OF THE WORLD
BICKLETON

Bickleton is for the birds. Bluebirds, specifically. Birdhouses out-
number human lodgings in this rural wheat-faming community,
which is what inspired its nickname of "Bluebird Capital of the
World." Bickleton's fields are located 20 miles north of the
Columbia River, and thousands of feathered friends come to
visit each spring. If you decide to join them, there's a new B&B

named the "Hen's Nest," for your own roosting pleasure.
Bickleton also features the curios Whoop-N-Holler Museum,
which displays pioneer memorabilia and such oddities as an old-
time horse-drawn hearse and an electric lunch box.

HANFORD RESERVATION
RICHLAND

The biggest nuclear-waste dump in the Western Hemisphere is
in Washington. Lucky us. Fifteen hundred residents were evicted
from the village of Richland so the top-secret Manhattan Project
could take over the site. The project built the world's first
industrial-scale nuclear reactor, the B Reactor, at the Hanford
Reservation in Richland during World War II. It produced the
plutonium for the Fat Man atomic bomb that exploded on
Nagasaki on August 9, 1945, with a blast the equivalent of 21,000
tons of TNT. The war ended. Victory was ours. But it left a
nightmare of contamination in its wake. The site encompasses
586 square miles, including 50 miles of the Columbia River.
Nuclear tanks leaked and radioactive particles seeped into the
water and blew over the soil. Fear that Hanford would become
the next Chernobyl put the last remaining reactor out cold in
1988, shutting it down completely three years later. Government
site directors candidly describe their present mission as the "largest waste cleanup effort in world history," as they struggle to contain and treat 25 million cubic feet of solid radioactive waste.

Shirley Olinger, manager of the Office of River Protection,
posts regular updates on the progress of the cleanup on the organization's website. Three million gallons of liquid were removed
from underground storage tanks to prevent leakage. A waste
treatment plant is being built to vitrify tank waste into glass.
Additional waste is being retrieved as you read this. Billions of
dollars are being spent to clean up the site, but concerns remain.
One recent study linked an increase in thyroid disease to those

living near Hanford when radioactive iodine still electrified the air. Radioactive tumbleweeds and ants also have been found. Conspiracy theorists wonder whether contamination from Hanford is responsible for Washington's unusually high incidence of multiple sclerosis and other autoimmune illnesses…but nothing has been proven.

Meanwhile, Richland has been restored and seems to be making the best of it. The buildings remain as a memorial to the Cold War era; a museum is being planned around the B reactor; and Richland calls itself the "Atomic City." The high school sports team is the Richland Bombers, and since 1945, their lettermen jackets have featured a big mushroom cloud on the back. Bomber T-shirts have become a collector's item, bringing in as many orders from tourists as from alumni.

ARCHIE MCPHEE
SEATTLE

Under the category of weird and wacky is the Archie McPhee shop. The shop, which is located on Market Street in the Ballard neighborhood in Seattle, calls itself the "Outfitters of Popular Culture"—others just say it's a stop you really shouldn't miss. Among the 10,000 items displayed throughout the store are bobble heads, devil duckies, mannequins, yodeling pickles and even a zombie spinner that asks "What would a zombie do?" and offers assorted options with the simple spin of a severed arm. The idea for the store actually came about when Archie McPhee's nephew, who'd taken to selling collectables and oddities, couldn't seem to keep up with the demand of his customers back in L.A. He packed up and moved near his dear uncle who, according to all accounts, seemed to be a fun-loving kind of guy and was not only a positive influence but also a great namesake for the business.

That was back in 1983, and apparently the store, which started out in the Fremont district, grew to such a degree that in 1999 it moved to a larger building in Ballard. The McPhee staff calls their store a "Mecca for connoisseurs of the strange and exotic." And along with the wide assortment of retail temptations is an equally wide assortment of prices—you can walk away just five cents lighter in the pocket or make a major $1000 purchase if you choose. They even accept bridal registries. Either way, a visit to Archie McPhee's retail store promises more fun than a barrel of monkeys (which you can buy there) and really, isn't that in itself worth the trip?

HOLLAND IN WASHINGTON
LYNDEN

As Poulsbo is to Norway, Lynden is to Holland. A small community of Dutch immigrants settled here just south of the Canadian border in Whatcom County, western Washington, in the early 1900s. True to their roots, they started a huge dairy farm industry that continues today. And they brought their culture with them, too. Holland Days is celebrated each year the first weekend in May, bringing traditional costumes and wooden-clogged Klompen dancers to the center of town. Downtown's Front Street is reminiscent of a Dutch village, complete with a 72-foot-tall working windmill. Windmill de Wijn is unusual in that its rotating blades, traditionally wooden, are made of metal. Lights frame their picturesque outline at night. Beneath the windmill is the Dutch Village Mall, which has a 150-foot canal running through the middle, just like the streets in Amsterdam. The gift shop inside sells windmill tchotchkes alongside such Dutch treasures as the blue and white china from Delft.

On Front Street, Lynden Dutch Bakery is famous for its Krenten Bolles (raisin buns), and local supermarkets have sections devoted to Dutch food. If you're looking for "hutspot," it's here. The traditional potato dish is served on October 3 for the

Dutch holiday of Leidens Ontzet, which marks the anniversary of Spanish soldiers' departure from the city of Leiden in Holland during the Eighty Years' War. How about peppernoten ginger cookies for a proper Sinterklaas (yes, similar to Santa Claus) celebration on December 5? You'll find them in Lynden by the bagful.

Dutch is still spoken around Lynden. Nostalgic expatriates connect with their heritage while natives keep their traditions strong. These include family first and foremost, and the keeping of pristine homes with open windows (curtains are for those who have something to hide). But despite once holding the world record for most churches per square mile and per capita, and a subsequent reputation for being a wholesome small town, Lynden gained notoriety in 2005 upon discovery of the Lynden Drug Tunnel. It seems Canadian drug smugglers built a tunnel from a basement in peaceful Lynden to a greenhouse in Langley, British Columbia. The bust shocked many, as no one could conceive of criminal activity beneath such a placid surface.

True Lynden is exemplified not by that scandalous one-time headline, but by the town's guileless, earnest hospitality. A real Dutch treat in Lynden is the opportunity to spend the night inside the windmill. The Dutch Village Inn occupies the top three floors of the Dutch Village Mall. Six bedrooms are inside the body of the mill, each named for a different Dutch province. The light-drenched rooms are larger than you'd imagine, with hot tubs in each. And where else, besides Holland itself, would you be able to perch in a window seat 72 feet up and watch as the windmill's blades whir by? Read on for more very unique lodgings available in Washington.

BIG
GARGANTUAN &
RIDICULOUSLY
OVERSIZED

APPLE PIE WITH A TWIST
Wenatchee

The folks down in Wenatchee sure love their apples, and so they should. The first apple trees were planted in the area in 1872, and in the early 1900s the community and its surrounding countryside were already being called the "Home of the World's Best Apples." By 1902 the city started referring to itself as the "Apple Capital of the World," and they even erected a giant road-side sign laying claim to the fact. So it only stands to reason that Wenatchee residents would try to bake the world's largest apple pie—and in 1997 the community entered the *Guinness Book of World Records* for doing just that. According to Watlow (the company that supplied the oven used to bake the monstrosity), the residents of Wenatchee gathered 36,666 pounds of apples, 6000 pounds of flour, 4200 pounds of shortening, a pinch (160 pounds worth) of salt, 1200 pounds of water, 427 pounds of brown sugar and 52 pounds of cinnamon to create the mother of all apple pies. The end product measured 44 feet in length, was 24 feet wide, almost a foot deep and weighed 38,000 pounds, breaking the 1982 record set by residents of Chelsfield, England. That pie weighed a mere 30,115 pounds.

Weird Lodging

*When you visit Washington, your unusual accom-
modation options are endless. You can wind down
in a Dutch windmill, sleep 50 feet above the
ground in a grown-up tree house, stow away in
a historic red caboose, go native in a tepee—even
camp out in a waterbed in a tent on the sand!*

YOU SLEPT IN A *WHAT?*

CEDAR CREEK TREEHOUSE
ASHFORD

One of the world's top three "extreme hotels" according to the *Travel Channel,* is located in Ashford. This bed and breakfast is unlike any other—a grown-up treehouse 50 feet above the ground in a 200-year-old western red cedar tree. A suspension bridge leads you through 80 feet of forest to a five-story staircase, a private pathway to your nest in the trees. The bi-level, 16-by-16 foot cottage seems to float in the air, with only birds for neighbors. The woodland setting extends to the carved furniture and the architecture itself—a tree trunk juts through the center of the kitchen. Sunbeams and sweeping views of the mountains and creek surround you at every turn. The brand new Treehouse Observatory (aptly named the "Stairway to Heaven") presents breathtaking views from 100 feet up in an adjacent fir tree. Nature is literally at your front door.

The Cedar Creek Treehouse is divided into several rooms, like a miniature apartment, and includes a fully functioning bathroom, gas stove, icebox, 12-volt lighting, a hammock and two personal skylights…everything but the kitchen sink. No, wait, it's got that, too. It sleeps five adventurers. This cabin in the sky is 10 miles from the Nisqually River Entrance to Mount Rainier National Park, on the border of the Gifford Pinchot National Forest. Several couples have taken their wedding vows up in the tree and honeymooned in the treehouse, which the owners call "the ultimate love nest." They're right.

WELLSPRING SPA
ASHFORD

At the foot of Mount Rainier rests a woodland retreat, Wellspring Spa and Log Cabins. I make a point of running away to their perfectly appointed luxury log cabins several times a year, but a little known treat—and certainly their weirdest and wackiest choice of accommodations—hides in the woods among the trail behind the cabins. Here you'll find luxury camping for people (like me) who are afraid to camp. They're called Tents in the Tulles, "the northwest's most pampered camping opportunity." Three canvas-walled tent cabins hide in the woods along a forested trail. All have wood stoves and propane heaters to keep you cozy, along with private nearby bathrooms with a shower skylight. And each tent is modeled as its own little theme party.

Trails End offers a candlelit queen-size bed for hibernators who aren't quite ready to sleep on nature's floor. The Timbuktu African safari tent has a king-size waterbed draped with romantic Masai netting. My personal favorite is the Tropics—a little bit of Hawaiian paradise in Washington. The tent floor is lined with 6 inches of pristine white sand. A king-size, four-poster palm waterbed takes you "out to sea." Your host, Sunny, has thought of everything, even bedside brushes to sweep the sand off your sheets. It's a perfect transition to "real" camping for newbie Washingtonians and city folks.

Can't get into Cedar Creek Treehouse? Wellspring also offers its own treehouse version. Nestled between two fir trees 15 feet above ground is a room with a view built for two and an outdoor "green room."

RED CABOOSE GETAWAY
SEQUIM

Why settle for staying on the right side of the tracks when you can stay on the tracks themselves? No, not in the tied down, damsel-in-distress style, but in your own comfortably appointed, cozy, private caboose. All aboard!

This little gem on Old Coyote Way in Sequim sits on Olympic Discovery Trail near Lavender Farms. The unique caboose lodgings have been lauded in papers as far away as the *San Francisco Chronicle*, the *New York Times* and even *The London Times*, but they still retain a homespun charm. There are four getaway cars to choose from, each with its own theme, from the Casey Jones conductor car to the Circus caboose. One of the favorites is the Orient Express, which recreates the romance of the rails with a whirlpool for two, a gas fireplace, hardwood floors, a queen feather bed and luxurious robes—the better to snuggle you with, my dear. The bed and breakfast is reinvented as passengers board a vintage 1937 Zephyr dining car, "The Silver Eagle," for a gourmet breakfast served by stationmasters Charlotte and Olaf. This wild ride is a lot more fun than your basic, boring hotel.

INDIAN SUMMER
MOUNT RAINIER

Visitors wanting to "do as the Natives do," or did, can stay in a tepee on the banks of Copper Creek. Indian Summer offers a solitary secluded tepee 2 miles from the Nisqually entrance of Mount Rainier National Park. The tepee can sleep up to four on a carpeted floor covered with comfy sleeping pads that blanket a bed of cedar bark. Enclosed in the tepee is a wood-burning stove to keep you warm, heat your tea or cook up a meal. Your personal fire pit waits just outside. You don't have to go completely native, though—a restroom and shower are right up the trail, as is the homestyle Copper Creek Inn Restaurant. The 6.5-acre property is also home to an art studio and forest retreat.

THE EDGEWATER HOTEL
SEATTLE

Starstruck music fans will want to stop by the Edgewater Hotel in Seattle. The luxury waterfront hotel definitely earns its name, as it floats on the edge of Elliott Bay. It's one of many hotels built in Seattle in 1962 to accommodate travelers to the World's Fair. But the Edgewater hosted some special guests. The Beatles stayed in Room 272 when they played Seattle on their first-ever American tour in 1964. The Famous Four took the hotel up on its unique offer to fish out their seaside room's window, immortalized in a famous photograph that hangs in the room where it happened. Guests can sleep where the Beatles slept, in a 700-square-foot studio-style suite decked out with a state-of-the-art stereo system (equipped with Beatles CDs, of course).

BIG

GARGANTUAN & RIDICULOUSLY OVERSIZED

WORLD'S LARGEST EGG
Winlock

If you're traveling through Winlock and pass Kerron and First streets, it won't take you long to guess what the town is famous for. That's right, since October 23, 1923, when the town first made the announcement, Winlock has boasted having the "World's Largest Egg." Of course, we're talking the fake variety here, but the original canvas egg, measuring 11 feet in length and hoisted on a 10-foot pole, was first conjured up as an appropriate town mascot because of Winlock's designation at the time of being the second largest egg-producing town in the country. Although that claim to fame may no longer hold true, the town is still mighty proud of its egg, so much so that the roadside attraction has undergone at least three facelifts. In 1944 it was converted from, by then, a tattered canvas egg to an egg made of plastic, and in 1960 it was remade out of fiberglass. Eventually even this model needed a facelift, so in 1993 a new fiberglass egg was built. And after more than eight decades standing proud in a city with a land base of a little over one square mile, it's not about to find itself tossed into the frying pan anytime soon!

Strange Structures

There are some structures out there, like the Grand Coulee Dam for example, which by their very mammoth size demand attention. You can't help but ask all the normal questions. Such as, how long did it take to build and how much concrete did they need, anyway? And when you get your answers, they'll blow you away, leaving you gob-smacked. In other cases, the questions you ask will be a little more basic. Such as, why on earth would someone spend all that time and money to create such an artistic masterpiece and then leave it in the middle of nowhere surrounded by a whole lot of rattlers? Whether it's an engineering marvel or kind-hearted gesture built to save squirrels from becoming road kill, you just have to see the structures and learn everything you can about the story behind them.

MAN-MADE MARVELS

COLUMBIA CENTER
(AND AMERICA'S BEST BATHROOM)
SEATTLE

Let's test your memory. Which Washington landmark measures 997.36 feet in height, boasts 1.5 million square feet of office space, and cost a mere $200 million to build from 1982 to 1985? If you guessed the Columbia Center, the Columbia Seafirst Center, the Columbia Tower, the Bank of America Tower or BankAmerica Tower in Seattle (or BOAT as some called it), you'd be right on all counts. That's because they are one in the same building—and the various names weren't the only thing that caused controversy. There were those who applauded developer Martin Selig for knowing how to make the best of an old and seemingly outdated building code system. And then there were others who criticized the development for its poor public amenities and for its negative impact on the environment. Still others outright condemned Selig's motivation, such as the late Victor Steinbrueck, who at the time spoke as a preservationist and Dean of the University of Washington School of Architecture. He was quoted as saying, "It's terrible. A flat-out symbol of greed and egoism. It's probably the most obscene erection of ego edifice on the Pacific Coast."

To be fair, as of this writing, the building only ranked 18th on the list of the nation's tallest 100 buildings, and it gets bumped down that list on a fairly regular basis. Compare the building to others in the world and it's even less noteworthy. But when it comes to the state of Washington, in fact any place west of the Mississippi River, the building towers above most others. It is the tallest in Washington, second tallest on the West Coast and is now fourth tallest west of the Mississippi, down from the first-place standing it held when it was built.

The controversial structure is actually composed of three U-shaped arches that give it the appearance of three separate towers. Because architects weren't allowed to take the Columbia Center to its full, original 1005-foot blueprinted height, only 76 floors are above ground, with another seven stories tucked away below terra firma. Developer Martin Selig asserted that the skyscraper "tells people Seattle has arrived." For those city dwellers who think that they, too, have arrived, the elite Columbia Tower Club occupies the top two stories of the building.

The members-only club also boasts a curious distinction: America's Best Bathroom. It's unclear who does the inspection and rankings (and you thought *your* job was bad) of these bathrooms, but the reasons are clear on why the club won out. The Columbia Club ladies room is a throne with a view. All the way up on the 76th floor, each of the four private stalls has its own floor-to-ceiling window with a spectacular view of the Cascade Mountain range. But don't worry, it's so high up that the only one invading your privacy would be an errant bird. Locals know that the best views of the city skyline aren't at the top of the Space Needle (which costs $16); they are at the tower's observation deck on the 73rd floor (for free). You can almost literally see forever—and you can most certainly watch the planes getting ready to land at the nearby Sea-Tac Airport.

On a more macabre note, the National Commission on Terrorist Attacks Upon the United States, also known as the 9/11 Commission, released its report on July 22, 2004, on the events leading up to and surrounding the September 11, 2001, attacks. On its list of intended targets were the "tallest buildings in California and Washington State," which means that Columbia Center and all its inhabitants might have faced the same fate as did those in the Twin Towers in New York City.

CHURCH OF GOD-ZILLAH
ZILLAH

It started out as a cute coincidence. Folks in the small town of
Zillah (named for Miss Zillah Oakes, the daughter of T.F.
Oakes, the president of the Northern Pacific Railroad), formed
a church. It was named the Church of God, and the church was
in Zillah. Therefore, it was the Church of God, Zillah. When
folks laughed at the name, and tourists started coming around
to take pictures of the church sign, the parishioners saw an
opportunity to save more souls. We can work with it, they real-
ized, and attract more people to our church to hear our sermons.

Minister Gary Conner also saw a new way to reach children and make Christianity cool: give them a mascot. The church adopted Godzilla and said, "We got him saved." A 10-foot figure of the dragon-like monster guards the parking lot, holding a big cross and a sign that says "Jesus Saves." He is also crowned with more than 3000 Christmas tree lights. The 175 regular church-goers hope this symbol shows the surrounding community that the faithful can be reverent and irreverent at the same time. They say their church is fun, and it even has hula-hooping in Sunday school. "We're not a bunch of stuffy people," says a member of the congregation, wearing a T-shirt with a cartoon Godzilla breathing fire and waving a cross. I believe her.

LITTLE WHITE CHURCH
ELBE

Along the side of the road on Highway 7, just 13 miles from Mount Rainier, is one of the smallest churches in the nation. Evangelische Lutherische Kirche is its full name, but the church is so small that the words don't fit on it, so the founders had to settle for "Ev. Luth. Kirche." The tiny structure, built in 1906 by settlers from Germany, measures only 18 feet by 24 feet, with a 46-foot steeple. The six rows of pews accommodate 50 wor-shippers at the most. Monthly services run from March through November, and in the tradition of Elbe's early pastor, the bishop arrives for summer service riding a bicycle. The church made the national register of historic places in 1976 and once appeared on "Ripley's Believe It or Not" as "the smallest church in America." It's also a popular site for weddings—as long as they're small.

YELLOW CHURCH CAFÉ
ELLENSBURG

If a long church service leaves you hungry for more tangible sustenance, check out the Yellow Church Café in Ellensburg for meals such as St. Benedict's Eggs, Morning Glory Cobbler and—you guessed it—the Last Supper. The café is run by preacher's children and serves up "fun, food, and fellowship" in a preserved German Lutheran church that was built in 1923.

WAYSIDE CHAPEL
SULTAN

The wayward can worship on the wayside of Stevens Pass Highway, at the Wayside Chapel. It's the spiritual equivalent of a rest stop, with a sign that invites travelers to "Pause…Rest… and Worship." The tiny church is 7 feet by 9 feet and is stuffed with four two-person pews and a narrow pulpit. Nothing grandiose, just a little God on the go.

SEATTLE PUBLIC LIBRARY— CENTRAL LIBRARY
SEATTLE

Seattle takes reading seriously. As our nation's most college-educated city, it has more bookstores per capita than anywhere else in the U.S., and by far the largest percentage of library cardholders. Did you know that Nancy Pearl, the inspiration behind that cool librarian action figure—"with real shushing action"— works here?

An undisputed epicenter of technology, Seattle has been lauded as the city with the best wireless Internet access in the United States. It's no wonder we pour our resources into a high-tech work of art for our city's Central Library branch.

The Seattle Public Library's Central Library on Fourth Avenue was designed by Pulitzer Prize–winning Dutch architect Rem Koolhaas in 2004. It immediately inspired a gushing love letter from the *New York Times* for its sleek, geometric glass, mesh and metal structure and post-modern décor. Tourists gawk, and locals flock. The library attracts more than 8000 visitors per day. A unique user-friendly design—book spirals on floating platforms—is complemented by lively modern colors. Canary yellow escalators lead you to a womb-like reading room painted lipstick red, another room hot pink, and yet another, cool lime. Bamboo and hardwood line the floor. Pendant lamps on the first floor dangle like they're in a hip bar, while cushy reading rooms contain subtle lights twinkling above like stars in the night sky. Lush indoor landscaping and an actual fountain set a scene of tranquility.

And though it may be a place for books, the Central Library takes full advantage of Seattle technology. A bank of 145 high-speed computers offers catalog and Internet access, and librarians wearing headsets rush around in constant communication. Yet this thoroughly modern structure is sustainable in Seattle's socially conscious "green" manner, achieving silver certification by the U.S. Green Building Council's Leadership in Energy and Environmental Design program. It's about as perfect as a library can get, even in your wildest imagination—a true source of civic pride. And it's sure to keep Seattleites busy reading for years to come.

BILL GATES' HOUSE
MEDINA

No, you can't visit the home of the richest man in the world, whose net worth tops $56 billion, but you can read and dream. Microsoft entrepreneur Bill Gates and his wife Melinda live in exclusive Medina, on the east side, across the bridge from Seattle. Their 50,000-square-foot complex is built on a hillside and is valued at $147.5 million. This is probably the most technologically advanced home on earth. The 5.1 acres encompass a pool, a trampoline room, a 20-seat theater and 100 computers that customize the lights, temperature and music to each resident's individual desires. (Guess they don't fight over the thermostat like mere mortals.)

BIG
GARGANTUAN & RIDICULOUSLY OVERSIZED

BOEING PLANT
Everett

The world's largest building is the Boeing assembly plant in Everett, Washington. The factory is so large that it has its own fire department, medical clinic and water treatment plant, and the workers get from place to place on bicycles. The aircraft factory stretches over 98.3 acres—that's bigger than the core of California's Disneyland, and magic is created at the factory, too. All of the Boeing 747, 767 and 777 planes are assembled indoors. Boeing is the largest manufacturer of commercial jetliners and military aircraft combined, and the company supplies a vast majority of the industry jobs in the Puget Sound region. And that's no surprise, given that a single 747 contains six million parts, almost one for every person in the state.

KEEPING IT UNDER WRAPS
UNDERGROUND SEATTLE

Imagine if the road you trod wasn't solid ground. If the house where you slept and the shop where you conducted your daily business wasn't completely what it seemed. What if beneath the city you know lay a place where other goings-on, hidden from light, were more sinister, and all that separated you from its clutches was the thinly veiled illusion that there was nothing there but mud and stone. There was a time when opium dens, illegal gambling houses and other businesses of questionable repute operated in Seattle, hidden from sight in the middle of the city.

It all started in 1889 when a hot pot of glue ignited a fire, which spread and ultimately destroyed 33 city blocks. At the time, the city fathers thought that rather than bulldoze and rebuild on soft ground that was prone to flooding, they'd simply fill it all in and build above. During the transition phase, before the streets were filled in and remade, some businesses may have already rebuilt from the roof of their previous establishment skyward, leaving patrons with the unsettling proposition of having to scale large ladders just to patronize their business of choice. Eventually, though, the landscape transposed itself into what looked like a normal business section once again, and the underground world, initially used by some shopkeepers for storage, was eventually abandoned. Or so it was thought. It wasn't long before the powers that be learned that many of the illegal activities they were working hard to curb above ground had moved underground. Homeless vagrants and even criminals looking to escape from the law were hiding out down below. Not only were law officials a little disgusted that the bad guys had found a new hiding place, but also that a secluded and sequestered area (like what was soon to be known as Underground Seattle) was a perfect breeding ground for diseases such as the bubonic plague.

So by 1907, every entry into Seattle's underground city was cordoned off and secured shut. And for a time it remained that way until, in 1965, businessman and entrepreneur Bill Speidel had a brainstorm. He thought that cleaning up at least a portion of the underground ruins and offering tours of the area would be an intriguing way to draw tourists to Seattle and, in the process, make some serious cash. And so he did just that, paying business owners located in Pioneer Square for the privilege of visiting their underground sites and developing a few additions of his own.

Today, folks are treated to a guided tour covering a three-block radius, and it comes complete with colorful tales of the darker side of Seattle history. So if you're in town and a buddy asks you if you'd like to trod up and down six flights of stairs to a place with poor lighting and uneven terrain, say yes. Chances are you're heading for Underground Seattle.

PIKE PLACE MARKET
SEATTLE

Ayeeeeya—Aarrrgh, Ayeeeeya—Aarrrgh. If you ever wander through the fish market portion at Seattle's Pike Place Market and hear a chorus of "Ayeeeeya—Aarrrgh," heed this word of warning—DUCK! Accompanying the chant-like groans of fishmongers stationed behind specialty counters are flying fish, and if you're not careful you might find yourself with a slap up-side the face and the addition of some rather smelly cologne. The tradition of tossing carp, salmon and even the slithery, slimy tentacle-heavy squid, started when John Yokoyama, owner of Pike Place Fish Market, bought the place in 1965. He'd already worked there for some time under the previous owner, who desperately hated his job and was looking for a way out. The man was so disillusioned with his work that after counting his steps from behind the counter to where he had to collect a pound of clams and back again, he turned to John and said, "Thirty-five

steps for a pound of clams." To hear John tell it, the work was drudgery for most everyone employed there, so when he took over he wanted to change all that, to lighten the mood. Increase the levity. And he started out by reducing the number of steps fishmongers had to walk by introducing another method of transferring goods—the good old overhand pass.

The fitness gurus among you might cry foul, pointing out all the health benefits of walking, but before you get too carried away, just think for a minute. Those salmon are pretty hefty and dead weight, pardon the pun. Toss and catch a few of these over an eight-hour shift and you won't need to lift weights to build your biceps. It's good for morale, too; tossing the fish seems to produce some sort of positive trickle-down effect. The practical jokes and ribbing that go on between staff and customers makes Pike Place Fish Market a great place to visit.

While the fish market portion of Pike Place has made itself famous the world over, the overall market draws a pretty healthy crowd as well. The market actually started out as a way for farmers to get fair market value for their products and provide consumers with reasonable prices. The first market was held on August 17, 1907, on the corner of First Avenue and Pike Street, and by 11:00 AM that same day, every vendor was sold out. It was a huge success that kept building throughout the years until it eventually moved to Seattle's downtown area, where it now occupies more than 9 acres, attracting in excess of 10 million visitors each year.

Along with the fishmongers, visitors can check out as many as 190 craft booths, 120 tables with farm produce, 240 street performers and musicians, as well as an assortment of neighborhood antique shops, restaurants and specialty stores. And if that's not enough to get you planning your next weekend outing, there's one more thing Pike Place Market is famous for. The world's first Starbucks is right here in Pike Place Market (1912 Pike Place), featuring the original logo of the bare-breasted mermaid, before her corporate makeover. Yes, this worldwide institution with more than 7100 stores in the U.S. and a presence in 37 foreign countries started right in Seattle, where this storefront opened in 1971. It's been satisfying coffee lovers ever since, and while Starbucks coffee is available just about everywhere, including several grocery outlets, if you're the nostalgic kind of person, you can sit for a spell and enjoy the taste and aroma in the first Starbucks store, which is still in business.

STONEHENGE
KLICKITAT COUNTY

Sam Hill was a little misguided when he set about building a monument to America's fallen World War I soldiers just outside of Maryhill, but what he accomplished will make your jaw drop nonetheless. Hill believed England's Stonehenge, which is on the list of UNESCO World Heritage Sites, was built as a ceremonial and sacrificial site of some sort, involving human victims. Hill's initial vision was to replicate that Stonehenge to remind the world how "humanity is still being sacrificed to the god of war."

Although his initial comparison didn't ring true, his masterpiece has evolved into a memorial that includes monuments for soldiers from the county who'd served and died in the great wars, as well as Korea and Vietnam. A dedication plaque erected at the site speaks of Hill's desire that the monument inspire those who visit it to "burn with that fire of patriotism which death can alone quench."

The monument was officially dedicated in 1918, but it was far from finished at the time. It wasn't until 1931 that the last stone was laid and the monument completed—just in time for Hill to see his masterpiece before he passed away. His remains are buried at the site.

Initially, Hill's Stonehenge was the central feature of the experimental Quaker community of Maryhill. Unfortunately, the town burned to the ground and all that remained was the stone monument. If that isn't odd enough for you, consider this: although the Maryhill Stonehenge is believed to be the first such replica in the U.S., it's certainly not alone—there are at least six others, and more are apparently popping up every day. There's one in Texas, New Mexico, Georgia and Michigan. Carhenge, located near Alliance, Nebraska, takes it's inspiration from Texas' very own Cadillac Ranch. Some of these gigantic sculptures are made with traditional rock and stone, whereas others are carved out of Styrofoam or built with old, discarded refrigerators; there are even inflatable varieties.

That said, does any of this make you wonder why folks would build these structures? Don't people have enough to do without constructing monstrosities for the likes of trivia writers and comedians everywhere to rant on and on about? The best explanation is found courtesy of Roadside America's website, which states that "the ancient megaliths must emit an invisible energy field powerful enough to enslave sculptors, builders and the odd guy with too much time on his hands."

SATSOP ABANDONED NUCLEAR PLANT
ELMA

This one will leave you scratching your head in wonder. It appears that in the 1970s, the Washington Public Power Supply System developed a plan to build develop two nuclear plants, one in Hanford and the other in Satsop. With a budget of $24 million, the Satsop plant was the largest project of its kind in American history. Construction began in 1977 and for the next few years carried on, tickety-boo, and then the unthinkable happened. Planners came up against a $961 million shortfall. Hmm. It goes without saying that you can't cough up that kind of change in short order. And so, in 1983 the project, 76 percent completed, sat vacant, aside from the workers responsible for the upkeep of the facility, waiting for the day when the money would be found. That never happened, and so in 1994, the last caretaker collected his final pay and the facility sat empty, as it still does to this day. But it does make for a rather interesting conversation piece.

There have been some changes to the area. The Grays Harbor Public Development Authority has redeveloped the site into a business and technology park, but if you are in the area and decide to have a look around, you can still see the two cooling towers left over from its earlier incarnation.

SEATTLE MONORAIL
SEATTLE

It hasn't been without its controversy, or calamity, but the Seattle Center Monorail, built for the 1962 World Fair, is still running the mile span between Westlake Center Mall and the Seattle Center. Each two-minute trip will cost you a couple of dollars—$4 for a return ticket—and as many as 200 passengers can climb aboard at any one time.

Although not exactly weird, there is one story behind the sale of the monorail that is a bit odd. It was originally built to shuttle visitors between the World Fairgrounds and downtown shops. It cost $3.5 million to build, but following the fair it was handed over, free of charge, to the Century 21 Corporation, which in turn sold it to the city for $600,000—a poor exchange for the original builders but a profit for Century 21. The Seattle monorail is the second oldest monorail in the country. It caught fire a few years ago but has been restored and is up and running once again.

NARROWS SQUIRREL BRIDGE
LONGVIEW

If I were in the market for a man and found Amos Peters on one of those "find your soul mate" websites, I wouldn't even need to meet him to know I was in love. Chances are when you hear what this man did, you'll feel the same way too.

Amos Peters was a builder who operated a construction company in Longview, with his offices near Olympic Way. From his window he could watch traffic come and go all day long, and in the process, he witnessed an endless number of fatalities. They weren't of the human variety, however; in fact, all the hit-and-run victims were squirrels, but Amos was still deeply affected. When he discovered a flattened squirrel with a nut still in its mouth, he was so moved that he decided to do something about it. In 1963, at a cost of $1000, dear Amos built a special bridge that spanned 60 feet from one side of Olympic Way to the other, just for the squirrels. It was jokingly dubbed "Nutty Narrows"—a name that became official with the erection of a sign on its underbelly—and before long folks noticed squirrels were using the bridge with increasing frequency, even teaching their young how to get across it. It garnered attention from media networks around the world, and in one article Peters was heralded in perhaps the most gracious way with the words: "Little men take time to cater to big people who might do them good. Only big men pause to aid little creatures." Twenty years after it was secured in place, the bridge was taken down and repaired. When it was raised up again, it was accomplished with great fanfare, attracting the attention of local dignitaries and the Disneyland celebrities Chip 'n' Dale and Mickey Mouse.

In a world where there just aren't enough people like Peters, the community bid him a final farewell in 1984. In his memory, a giant squirrel was carved and erected near Nutty Narrows.

GALLOPING GERTIE
TACOMA

The first Tacoma Narrows Bridge was the fifth longest suspension bridge in the country when it opened in July 1940. Only four months later, it achieved international fame for a different reason—its dramatic collapse. From the start, the bridge over Puget Sound, connecting Tacoma to the Kitsap Peninsula, exhibited challenges to its stability. Although it was shallow and aesthetically pleasing, insufficient support (8-foot girders, instead of the recommended 25-foot ones) left the bridge susceptible to wind. Even a mild wind current sent the bridge rolling several feet up and down in mere seconds, earning it the instant nickname "Galloping Gertie," for the movement it caused as it swayed. Some sought the phenomenon out, excited by the galloping motion and occasional disappearance of other cars from view.

But on November 7, 1940, the wind was too much for Gertie—and her passengers. The friendly rolling progressed to violent twisting, sending the bridge swinging 28 feet high. The roadway tilted 45° in either direction. The center section of the bridge dropped 195 feet below into the water. Half an hour later,

600 feet of the remaining bridge broke free, flipped upside down, and plunged down as well. Thankfully, no humans were killed in the collapse, though one small life was lost: Tubby the black-haired cocker spaniel went down in a car, and neither he nor the vehicle was ever found. A local resident, who happened to be the owner of a camera shop, caught the wreck on film. The Library of Congress selected the film for the U.S. National Film Registry for its historic significance. Galloping Gertie remains where she fell. Her wreckage is registered as a Historical Landmark, and an unofficial cautionary tale.

520 BRIDGE
LAKE WASHINGTON

And they think they do it big, deep in the heart of Texas! When it comes to having the longest floating bridge, Seattle has that state, and in fact any other place in the world, beat hands down! Washington State has three of the world's six floating bridges. The Evergreen Point Floating Bridge, or SR-520, is the longest floating bridge in the world at 7578 feet. It's also the heaviest.

The bridge was built to carry 65,000 vehicles per day between Seattle and the east side, home to Bellevue and Medina. That number has ballooned to 115,000 cars daily, and rush-hour traffic is particularly ugly, so 520 has become infamous among locals for also having some of the worst traffic jams. Luckily, Mother Nature compensates commuters with a breathtaking view of the Olympic Mountains. Surrounded by water on both sides, underneath the watchful eye of the glorious mountaintops, it's tough to succumb to road rage. But as it nears its fifth decade, 520 is vulnerable to earthquakes and windstorms.

Having learned its lesson from Galloping Gertie, the Department of Transportation is at work planning the SR 520 Bridge Replacement and HOV Project. The project will replace the aging bridge with a safer, more reliable structure built to withstand a 1000-year earthquake event and winds up to 92 miles per hour. By popular demand, two lanes (for a total of six) will be added to improve traffic. The plan is still in the preliminary stages, and construction bids won't be accepted until 2012, so in the meantime locals have to grin and bear it and remember that holding the title for longest floating bridge may sometimes mean a longer wait, too.

SOUTHWEST SPOKANE STREET SWING BRIDGE
SEATTLE

If we're speaking of bridges ranking world recognition, the Southwest Spokane Street Swing Bridge certainly can't be left out. Spanning the Duwamish River, linking the industrial portions of south and southwest Seattle to Harbor Island, the bridge was completed in 1991, and according to the Seattle Department of Transportation, is recognized as "the world's first and only hydraulically-operated concrete double-leaf swing bridge." (In case that's not enough to impress, each of the two leaves is 480 feet long and weighs 7500 tons!)

Seattle was pretty darned proud of its new bridge, and with the newly widened channel, large boats had an easier time of maneuvering through. But the wider engineering community was also impressed—so much so that the bridge has earned itself four different engineering awards including one from the Washington State Society of Professional Engineers in 1991 for Outstanding Engineering Achievement, and one from the American Society of Civil Engineers in 1992 for Outstanding Engineering Achievement. The bridge also received three additional awards from the Washington Aggregates and Concrete Association, the Portland Cement Foundation and the National Endowment for the Arts.

CASCADE TUNNEL
SCENIC

I think you have to be a little bit crazy to actually check out this off-road attraction, but if you do—and you survive the excursion—you should get a pretty good bang for your buck. Back when Washington State was just being developed, there were many transportation problems. In particular, it was difficult, if not impossible, to navigate around the mountains. And when you're building a railroad, that's kind of important. So the Great Northern Railway decided, in one particularly challenging area in the Cascade Mountains where train tracks made eight switchbacks, to do the most reasonable thing possible—and they needed a lot of dynamite to do it. Blowing through the rock and creating a railroad tunnel would get them from point A to point B a lot more efficiently, would protect the train from the elements and would reduce accidents caused by snow slides and avalanches.

Theoretically, it was a great idea. Construction on the first tunnel, which traveled through 2.6 miles of solid rock, began in 1897, and it was ready for rail traffic by 1900. Of course, as with any new project, there were a few glitches. Built at a fairly steep

grade, the tunnel had problems with poor air circulation and the subsequent build-up of fumes. Its location was also susceptible to snow slides. By 1925, construction for a longer tunnel began. The new tunnel measured 7.8 miles in length, ran a straight line between Berne and Scenic, and earned a reputation as the longest railroad tunnel in the country, until 1989. It was built at a lower elevation than the first tunnel, didn't struggle with the same poor air circulation because of the eventual addition of a ventilation system and was less apt to have the same problems with snow.

So now that you know all the ins and outs of this marvel of engineering—in 1993 it earned the distinction of being named a U.S. Engineering Landmark—it's time for the really weird stuff. Some sources suggest that, though the new tunnel is an amazing site to see, if you really want an amazing experience, you need to check out Cascade Tunnel number one. You have to be careful, though. It's been abandoned since 1929, so it's not in the best of shape. Flash floods in the area have caused a lot of damage and promoters of the Iron Goat Trail, which is a walking trail that eventually brings travelers to the old tunnel, warn visitors to stay out. In fact, they'd really like it if you stood back from the entrance at least 300 yards. If a flash flood should occur, the whole thing could collapse, and that would certainly detract from the kind of memorable experience you had in mind. You should also be warned that the area is thick with wildlife of the most dangerous kind. Even if you can't see them, bears, wolves, mountain lions and other creatures are there— and they can see you.

And then there are the ghosts. The tunnel is the site of the "deadliest avalanche in U.S. history and the fourth deadliest railroad disaster." At least 96 people died at the site in March 1910, and you can't tell me that the souls of all those accident victims calmly went off to meet their maker without a fight. So if you're looking for a weird, wild and outrageous experience, visiting the site some call the "creepiest location in America" has to make it to your top 10 list.

GRAND COULEE DAM
COLUMBIA RIVER

If you were to ask, most Americans would likely point out that the largest concrete structure in the country is the Grand Coulee Dam. And if you're someone who didn't know that, here are all the reasons why you should have.

Building the dam was a long process that started with the seed of an idea in the 1920s and wasn't a completely finished and operational dam until 1951, with ongoing construction continuing into 1975. It took 12 million cubic yards of concrete to build the structure—which according to some sources is enough concrete to build a four-lane highway, 4 inches thick, from Los Angeles to New York City, a total distance of 3000 miles.

Comparatively speaking, the Grand Coulee Dam is bigger than the Great Pyramid in Egypt—four times bigger. The Grand Coulee area chamber of commerce calls it the "Eighth Wonder of the World." A working hydroelectric dam, it produces 6.5 million kilowatts of power to folks living throughout the Pacific Northwest. (Incidentally, that makes it the third largest hydro-electric facility in the world.) The dam, which is located in central Washington, shares the Columbia River with 10 other dams.

RED RADIO FLYER WAGON
Spokane

Riverfront Park in downtown Spokane has a little something for everyone. Spanning more than 100 acres, the park boasts the typical bicycle paths and flowerbeds. Originally established for Expo '74, it's also well equipped with an opera house, IMAX Theater, a kiddy playground and one super-sized Red Radio Flyer Wagon. The wagon is 27 feet long and children can climb aboard using the ladder on one side and slide back to the ground on the other. Youngsters have a great time going up and down while their parents look on, feeling a little like a character in a Salvador Dali painting.

Weird Art

Art is in the eye of the beholder. One person's garbage is another person's masterpiece—or in some cases, one man's garbage is his own masterpiece. Washington is dedicated to art—so much so that Seattle was one of the first cities in the U.S. to adopt a percent-for-art ordinance in 1973. This law stipulates that one percent of city capital improvement funds must be devoted to public art. The program integrates artwork into public settings to the point where you can barely walk a block without tripping over something interesting and beautiful.

Because this is Washington and we have to do things our own way, this art sometimes takes strange forms. If you're interested in the offbeat, the bizarre, the good, bad and the sometimes ugly, one thing is for sure, Washington works to make art accessible to everyone, not just the upper echelon who studied it in art school.

ART IS IN THE EYE OF THE BEHOLDER

BETTIE PAGE HOUSE
SEATTLE

You can catch an eyeful driving north in Seattle on I-5. As you near the exit for NE 65th Street, be sure to glance to your right for a glimpse of pin-up icon Bettie Page. No, it's not Bettie in person. She lives in California and has better things to do than hang out by the highway recreating cheesecake poses from her infamous youth. Besides, she's 85 now. But you can see a 17-foot-tall mural of topless Bettie in thigh-highs stockings painted on the side of a house. The eaves are strategically placed, covering her breasts like a black censor line. The "Bettie Page house" is a private home in the Roosevelt neighborhood owned by Chris Brugos, who commissioned the work from artist John Green as a present to himself for his 30th birthday in 2006.

The painting is fully visible off the highway—and next to a Mormon Church—but still inspires more compliments than complaints. Strangers knock on Chris' door to compliment it. None of them are members of the Latter Day Saints' congregation, but a member of the church, Jerry Watt, summed up the local opinion: "live and let live."

JIMI HENDRIX STATUE
SEATTLE

Never let it be said that Seattle isn't a rocking place. If you need proof that we've got our groove on, just take a hike down Broadway in Capitol Hill and keep your eyes peeled. If you're observant, you'll catch a life-sized, bronze version of the rocker, guitar in hand, performing as if he were still alive. "Excuse me while I kiss this guy!"

GAS WORKS PARK SUNDIAL
SEATTLE

From the early 1900s to the 1950s, an old gasification plant powered much of Seattle. Its rusty remains lend Gas Works Park its name. At the top of Gas Works hill is an elaborately sculpted, 28-foot-wide, interactive sundial that enlists the viewer as part of the artwork. A plaque instructs you to cast your shadow, becoming the gnomon, or stylus, of the piece to tell the actual time. It's surprisingly accurate, as well as downright fun. Artists Charles Greening and Kim Lazare created the sundial in the late '70s using bronze, shells, ceramics and other objects they found. A circular brick path surrounds the timepiece, which is not only signed by the artists but also contains an imprint of Greening's feet for good measure.

SOUND GARDEN
SEATTLE

I never promised you a Sound Garden…but here it is. Doug Hollis' landmark outdoor wind harp in northeast Seattle's Magnuson Park is like a large, musical weathervane. When the sculpture's 12, tall, narrow organ pipes catch the wind, they emit an eerie, otherworldly moan. The movement of the wind turns each vane, pushing the metal pipes to produce the resonating sound. The hypnotic guttural chimes manage to be lilting and chilling all at once. The Seattle grunge band Soundgarden borrowed its name from the sculpture. Since 9/11, you can reach the sculpture only on foot through the National Oceanic and Atmospheric Administration access road in the park.

STATUE OF LIBERTY
ALKI BEACH

I thought the Statue of Liberty was in New York. Turns out she also makes an appearance at Alki Beach in West Seattle. This seven and a half foot tall replica of Lady Liberty was a gift to the city from Reginald H. Parsons and the Seattle Council of the Boy Scouts of America in 1952. It's a tourist attraction on a stretch of beach that pays homage to New York landmarks. Once called "The Coney Island of the West," Seattle's waterside amusement park at Alki Beach closed in 1913. All that remains is the Luna Park Café, named after New York's Coney Island Fairgrounds. When Seattle founders Arthur Denny and the Denny Party arrived at Alki Point in 1851, they named it "New York-Alki." *Alki* is a Chinook Indian word meaning "by and by," so they were essentially naming Seattle "New York Pretty Soon," indicating their hopes for the burgeoning city. It's New York enough in Alki, and we've got our own statue to prove it.

SELF-KICKING MACHINE
ROCKPORT

Rockport Country store found an unlikely way to attract customers—by giving them a kick in the pants! A self-kicking machine was placed in front of the store in the 1950s, and it's been entertaining curious visitors ever since. Blink and you'll miss Rockport, a speck on the map on Route 20 near Anacortes, but this little oddity is worth looking for. Interactive performance art of sorts, the machine is not for the easily embarrassed. You must bend over in the proper position, turn a crank and then stand still as the chain revolves to give you the boot. But please don't drop your pants. Rockport is a family town.

DICK & JANE'S SPOT
ELLENSBURG

Take a look around you. Chances are you'll notice people bustling about, here and there, in a big hurry to get something done. The world is full of Type-A personality folks: the diligent and responsible goal-centered individuals who are very competitive and don't know how to relax. Whenever they have a spare moment, they need to fill it with something constructive and productive—like doing dishes or a load of laundry—and for a good chunk of society it's been a long time since they've just sat down and enjoyed the world around them. It's a pretty sure bet that the people down at Dick & Jane's Spot in Ellensburg wouldn't understand this at all, and that's a good thing. If they were anything like the kind of person described above, they'd have never created the living masterpiece they call home.

For more than 25 years now, the couple has transformed ordinary fencing into canvasses that serve as a backdrop for everything from Jane's painted murals to Dick's reflector art.

Discarded objects have been recreated into sculptured art forms that have, many times, sent visitors off in gut-busting laughter— or at least with something to talk about throughout the day. The sun's rays bounce off the thousands of industrial grade reflectors, glass bottles, bottle caps and other light-catching materials, tossing color here and there while the wind Ellensburg is so well known for teases spinner trees into action. And that is just what visitors passing by can see. The interior of the couple's home provides a more private canvas for their work, along with the work of other artists they've collected through the years. Dick and Jane have also recreated their own Garden of Eden in their backyard, where every summer, wildflowers bloom, making their own magic and mingling with even more sculptures.

Everything is alive at Dick & Jane's Spot. It's a bit of heaven in the middle of the everyday grind. But trying to describe it to someone who's never been there is, in Dick's own words, "kind of hard to explain." In the couple's online video, Jane recalls one 10-year-old's perspective on the place. He asked, "Is this what you call imagination?" It's probably the best description the couple has ever had of their home.

When the couple started creating their living and changing art display, they knew they'd attract attention, and they even planned for it—a guestbook is displayed front and center and invites passersby to put down their thoughts, good or not so good. They've even set up a rating system on their website, offering surfers a chance to rate their artwork. So if you're ever in the neighborhood, stop by. And don't forget to tell them what you think.

CLUB LAGOON'S WHITE LAMBORGHINI
SEATTLE

Shoppers strolling down Capitol Hill's trendy alterna-street, Broadway, often stop to gawk at a white Lamborghini fixed onto the roof of a building at a precarious angle. "What the hell is *that*?" they demand. *That* is all that's left of Club Lagoon, a controversial *Miami Vice*-style nightclub that arrived brazenly with the car in 2006, and burned out within a year, amid cop calls and reports of violence. Local residents had it in for the club from the beginning, complaining that the car was too tacky for the neighborhood…until pragmatists pointed out that the shop beneath it was a neon Castle Superstore adult emporium. The car stayed. And though the club is now defunct, its pesky remnant remains. A white Lamborghini perched atop a building on a major street is tough to ignore. Art or eyesore? You be the judge.

RICHART'S ART YARD
CENTRALIA

When it comes to outdoor art, Dick and Jane certainly have company. In Centralia, Richard Tracy has been transforming his yard for more than 20 years, and by the looks of things, he's come a long way, baby! "RichArt"—as he prefers to be called—is a real character. He uses discarded objects to unleash his imagination and create his masterpieces.

What is known about this eccentric is that he taught at public school for 10 years and worked as a janitor at a home improvement store for another 30. It is well reported that he has a fixation with the number 5: he offers 5 free minutes of his time to visitors, but if they want to talk any longer they must pay him

$5 and he'll go on for another 55 minutes; he's been known to offer an option to the $5 tour and allow visitors into his studio to create their own unique art for 55 minutes; and when he dies he's instructed the executor of his last will and testament to wait 5 days and then call one of his friends, who conveniently has a bulldozer, and instruct him to plow down all his creations—and his friend has 5 hours to do so. His art has been known to bring people to tears, but at the same time, some folks are a little leery of the fellow. One visitor told of her overwhelming fear of the man when she first met him, but now she can't wait to visit RichArt's Art Yard again.

RichArt appears to have a bit of a cubist influence in some of his sculptures, all of them reflect the shape of the items used to build them, and his use of metal certainly adds depth to the art forms under different degrees of sun and moon light.

Already into his 70s, RichArt doesn't appear to be slowing down any. Several people visit his outdoor art display each day and between interacting with them, scavenging for more inspirational bits and pieces, and creating his art, this is one fellow who knows how to live life to the fullest!

RECYCLED SPIRITS OF IRON
MOUNT RAINIER

Art lovers looking for something a little different in the midst of their wilderness travels in Mount Rainier National Park might want to check out the work of artist Dan Klennert. Just outside of Elbe and right near Mount Rainier's west entrance, along State Route 706, is Ex-Nihilo Sculpture Park. The term "Ex-Nihilo" was first coined by a visitor who, on touring Klennert's collections of metal sculptures, repeatedly muttered the phrase. Translated, the Latin term means "something made out of nothing," and because it so completely describes what Klennert does—creating art from castoff metal and discarded objects—Ex-Nihilo became part of the park's name.

The park boasts an eclectic assortment of sculptures representing everything from creatures of the sea to dinosaurs, animals and people who, like the Angel from Hell, look like they'd seen better days. There's an eerie ghostliness to the sculptures that Klennert says come to life in his mind by their very form as they lay on the discard pile. To Klennert, they look like parts of the anatomy of a giraffe, a seahorse or a roadrunner, and so in his talented hands that's what his recycled "spirits of iron" become.

While much of his work is on permanent display at the park, Klennert does travel throughout the U.S. and into Canada with some of his sculptures. And many of his works have been sold to private collectors.

Klennert welcomes visitors to stop by and say hello when visiting the park. I'm thinking that getting to know a little bit about the man, who, at age of seven, started collecting junk and turning it into art, can only enhance your appreciation for his work.

METAL PEOPLE
RAYMOND

In keeping with making art out of metal, the folks in the small town of Raymond, population 3000, have enhanced their town with scenes celebrating the community's heritage, as well as the area's wildlife. The idea for the project seemed to take root in 1993 when a group of artists decided to produce works of art that told some of the history of the area. Made of metal, which over the years had rusted enough to look like wood, the statues have a slightly eerie quality to them. Turn a corner and you might spot a statue of a youngster feeding a squirrel. Around another corner you might bump into elk or bears or scenes of loggers loading a wagon. Some sculptures resemble the town's locals, such as the sculpture erected in honor of Raymond's World War II hero Robert Bush.

If you travel the Raymond Wildlife Heritage Sculptures Corridor or venture downtown and you see a sculpture that captures your imagination like no other, chances are you can take a replica home with you for a nominal fee. You can find these replicas at the local chamber of commerce.

METAL HORSES
VANTAGE

When you're driving along Interstate Highway 90, near Vantage, look to the hills. In the distance you'll notice what looks like a herd of horses, some rearing up on their back legs and others running forever, and yet going nowhere. These horses were sculptured by artist David Govedare from metal and are a legacy to an Native American creation legend that tells of how the "Grandfather Spirit" breathed life into the area and lowered a basket filled with ponies that were supposed to "inspire a Spirit of free will." If you've ever been to the site, you're likely scratching your head right about now, wondering where the basket, which in the legend represents the Grandfather Spirits heart, went. The Thundering Hooves Sculpture Committee, the group responsible for the sculpture that is called "Grandfather Cuts Loose the Ponies," is still trying to raise the funds needed to build it. Last I heard, they're still taking donations.

In the meantime, the horses are a wonder to see, and visitors are encouraged. However—and this is a big however—they are located in an area where there's a huge population of rattle-snakes, so tread carefully!

METAL COWS
OLYMPIA

This one is an odd entry, to be sure. You can't pass by it without at least a cursory glance. You see, there are reports on Roadside America and other tourist websites that in a field just off Highway 101, somewhere not far from Olympia, you might notice a bull in mid-rush and a mother cow and her calf, which, in and of itself, is not unique at all. However, if you pause along the side of the highway, even just for a moment or two, it won't take long before it hits you that they aren't moving. In fact, they aren't even breathing. These cows, so lifelike that they easily confuse passing motorists, are actually metal sculptures.

Now, if you trace their movements, you'll notice they've moved around a bit before ending up where they are at the writing of this book. Of course, there's no guarantee they'll not move again. No one seems to know where they came from or who's responsible for their creation. With this roadside attraction, you get a two-for-one deal—a photo op and a great mystery!

OLYMPIC STRUCTURE PARK
SEATTLE

Progress is necessary to the development of any community, and in 1910, the promise of progress showed itself in a big way for Seattle when the Union Oil Company of California (UNOCAL) established a transfer and distribution facility on its waterfront. The company did its business from that base until 1975, and when the site was decommissioned, UNOCAL spent a full 10 years—until 1999—cleaning up the land. That's when the Seattle Art Museum, in partnership with the Trust for Public Lands, set out to buy the property. Their goal was to preserve what, by that time, was the city's last, undeveloped waterfront property. It cost $16.5 million just for the land, but its current value to Seattle is priceless. Beginning in 2002, plans were drawn up to reclaim the area for parkland. Dirt was dumped at the site, and by 2005 construction begun. One year later, the site was ready to begin installing some of the sculptures that, if you're an art lover, might be your main draw to the area.

Weiss/Manfredi Architects designed the park with a vision to "transport art outside the museum walls and bring the park into a landscape of the city." To do that, they've incorporated Seattle's cityscape as a structural backdrop to a park that blends modern and futuristic sculpture with plants and landscapes native to the Pacific Northwest. A 2200-foot-long, zigzag path of crushed stone intersects the parkland, leading visitors from sculpture to sculpture, and if you're looking to take a break and digest the meaning behind Bunyan's Chess Set, Persephone Unbound, the Riviera or any of the other 20-something pieces, check out one of the more experiential pieces and take a seat on one of the assorted eyeball benches or Roy McMakin's cement-sculpted furniture. Olympic Sculpture Park opened to visitors in January 2007, and if you've yet to check it out, it's located on 2901 Western Avenue in Seattle.

INDIAN PAINTED ROCKS

YAKIMA

Just outside of Yakima, at the intersection of Powerhouse and Ackely Roads, you enter a world that echoes of yesterday. Covering a small land area as far as parks go, Indian Painted Rocks is about 2000 square feet of primarily rock. This is where earlier civilizations etched out their stories in pictographs and petroglyphs. There's a lot that's unclear about their origin, or

even how long ago they were painted on the basalt cliffs overhead, but some estimate they date back more than 1000 years. The pictographs are found along an old trail that was frequented by the Yakima Indians in earlier times, but even they aren't completely sure the origins of these 80-plus paintings. Comparisons have been drawn between these pictographs and those found elsewhere in the western United States and Canada, and it is thought some of these ghostly images in white tell of hunts and meetings between tribes. To look at them, you are almost transported to another time, face-to-face with the first founders of this fair land.

Sadly, many of the pictographs have been destroyed with graffiti, damaged beyond repair or moved from the site altogether, but plans are in works to protect those that remain so that any additional graffiti can be easily removed.

WOODEN FISH
SEKIU

It's really tiny, but for anglers who've ever fished its waters, it's as memorable as that first kiss. Originally established to house workers in the salmon-canning, leather-tanning and logging industries, the community of Sekiu is still unincorporated. But today, it's mostly known as a tourist destination, with fish as the prime draw. Even if you're not into fishing, you'll recognize the town's claim to fame by its mascot—the carved wooden statue of a fish girl. With the head and upper body of a fish, you know it's a girl by its bikini top, pink skirt and running shoes. Perhaps the message here is that the fish are as alluring as a gorgeous young lady?

CODGER POLE
COLFAX

Americans really love football. I mean *really* love football. So much so that arguments over the merits of a game played between rival teams can be debated for many, *many* years. Such was the case with the 1938 meeting between the Colfax and St. John high school teams. Whatever happened during that fateful match, it certainly didn't end with the final score. Fifty years later, in 1988, both teams played a rematch game (starring all the original players who were by then somewhere in their 60s) to iron out their differences and erase any doubts as to who, indeed, was the best team.

The legacy they left behind this time is the largest sculpture of its kind in the world. Four poles measuring 65 feet in height sport caricature-like images of the 52 players involved in the original game. Master carver Jonathan LaBenne completed the sculpture using a chainsaw, and while each individual is wearing his football gear, the players are pictured as the seniors they were at the time of the rematch and not the strapping young lads they once were. The Codger Pole is fittingly located in Codger Park.

BIG
GARGANTUAN & RIDICULOUSLY OVERSIZED

WORLD'S LARGEST FRYING PAN
Long Beach

Wayward husbands beware! Push things a little too far and that wife of yours might finagle some way of using this Long Beach roadside attraction to teach you a lesson or two. Located directly across from Marsh's Free Museum is what folks in these parts call the World's Largest Frying Pan. As with most landmarks of this type, there is a story behind the odd sculpture. It was apparently erected on July 24, 1931, in celebration of the Farmers-Merchants Picnic.

Ghost World

Whole books could be written on the many ghosts that (supposedly) populate Washington State—in fact, they have been. So here I'll just highlight my favorites: the weirdest and wackiest of the supernatural world. Whether you're a diehard believer or a scepter skeptic, these tales of Washington's spooky spirits are enough to raise the hair on the back of your neck or at least make you wonder.

Some ghosts are harmless and humorous. Others are chilling, like the 100-step staircase in Greenwood Cemetery in Spokane Falls that no one can scale without being overcome by an unbearable feeling of fear. Washington's even has its own ghost busters. Their approach is scientific—they arrive equipped with gadgets used to detect seismic activity, heat, energy and the voices of ghosts.

PHANTASTIC PHANTOMS

CLAREMONT HOTEL
SEATTLE

The ghosts on the ninth floor of Seattle's Claremont Hotel have some ghastly manners. They seem permanently stuck in a prohibition party zone. Hotel employees have heard sounds of a raucous party from the prohibition era with period music, loud laughter, arguments and the sound of glass breaking. Hotel guests have noticed it, too, often calling the front desk to complain about the noise and to ask them to turn it down. But as a former staff member says, "How do you turn off a ghost?" Their way of dealing with the disturbance has been to go up to the ninth floor to investigate, even though they know no one's there. When they arrive, the noise suddenly stops. Of course, as soon as they're out of eyeshot, the ruckus starts right up again.

THE CAPITOL THEATER
YAKIMA

If you're partial to benevolent ghosts, you'll like beloved Shorty, the friendly ghost at the Capitol Theater in Yakima. For 50 years, Shorty has been accepted as part of the theater's scenery. Supposedly there's a door backstage 12 feet up the concrete wall known as "Shorty's door." Sometimes it's ajar, though there's no ladder beneath it. Paranormal experts called in for a look detected a hot spot 12 feet in the air at the front of Shorty's door. Whether it's real or mere theatrics, the stories about Shorty are quite dramatic. He's an ornery fellow. You pull the curtains up, he brings them back down. You open the green room door, he decides he prefers it closed. The stage goes dark as it should, but then the lights come back on, without human help. Light designer Moe Broom swears it was Shorty who once turned on the work lights when he was a few feet away from the switch. And the ushers tire of his joke of pulling all the audience seats down, right after they put them up.

But Shorty's most acclaimed performance was when he was credited with saving an actress' life. A stagelight shutter came apart and was falling toward the girl's head. It moved abruptly and visibly to the side and hit the stage instead. You can either blame it on some weird physics, or you can believe there might be something to this Shorty business. For a ghost, Shorty is pretty human. He even flushes the toilet when no one else is near the commode. Although you'd never suspect that ghosts have bodily functions, at least this one cleans up after his invisible self.

HARVARD EXIT THEATER
SEATTLE

What is it with ghosts and theaters? Capitol Hill's landmark Harvard Exit Theater on Roy Street was once the Women's Century Club, a gathering place in the 1920s for Seattle's earliest feminists. It seems the women may be reluctant to leave the comfort of the building. In the '70s, manager Jane Wainright was always the first one to open the theater. Sometimes she would unlock the building to discover a fire already lit and burning in the fireplace. The lobby chairs would have been moved into a circle around the fire, as if for some fireside chats. This happened with some regularity for years, even though Jane was the only one with the keys. Jane says she's seen three different women in the lobby, most notably a woman with an elegant upswept hairdo, wearing a long gown reading in a chair in the lounge. She wouldn't have thought anything of it, except that the woman was transparent. Jane was validated when, years later, a projectionist arrived at his job to find a movie already playing without his assistance. He readied himself to open the door to catch a prowler in the act, but the door was locked. When he finally got it open with his key, he was surprised to find the room empty.

Most of the sightings occur on the theater's third floor. Moviegoers have reported hearing mysterious laughter. Others report seeing an apparition of a hanged woman crying from the ceiling in the hallway. Many describe the same tall elegant woman, reclining in a chair, sometimes looking up from her book to acknowledge the flesh and blood person who is staring at her.

THORNEWOOD CASTLE
LAKEWOOD

One of Washington's most legendary haunts is the grandiose Thornewood Castle. Built in 1911, the 54-room castle has copious otherworldly activity. Gigi, the mother of the castle's owner, reports that lights have been observed unscrewing themselves from their sconces in builder Chester Thorne's room after his demise. His wife Anna has been spotted at her window seat overlooking the sunken garden. She is visible only in the reflection from the mirror. A pale, white-haired child has been seen going into the office but disappears when the door is opened. Saddest of all is the ghost of another owner's grandchild, who drowned in the nearby lake. Concerned guests ran from the Grandview Suite to the lake to help the small child alone by the water, but when they got there, the child had vanished.

The stately castle is on the National Register of Historic Places, and guests continue to add to its uncommon legacy. A visiting mother and daughter recorded their experience in the rooms' journals. The mother joked that one of the women in a hallway painting was ugly. She and her daughter both felt an urgent need to apologize, and did. But when they passed the painting again on their way back to their room, the mother slipped and fell. The daughter laughed, and then she fell, too, but caught herself before falling down the stairs. Both blamed the picture. Washington State's Evergreen Paranormal Group pays frequent visits to the castle, thought to be a hotbed of paranormal activity. Meanwhile, Steven King's "Rose Red" mini-series was filmed here in 2002…talk about scary!

THE MISSING KLICKITAT CHILDREN
YACOLT

Yacolt is the Native American word for "haunted place." Klickitat legend tells that a small band of Natives in what is now Clark County mysteriously lost their children while picking huckleberries in the woods. The children strayed away from the camp and were never seen again. After a desperate and futile search, the Klickitat concluded that the evil spirit Yacolt had stolen them. The region was thought to be alive with evil spirits, devouring children whenever they came near.

GLENACRES GOLF COURSE
SEATTLE

It sort of makes sense that if Glenacres Golf Course is indeed an ancient Native American burial grounds, a spirit may remain. Many people have described seeing the same figure over the course of 20 years. He was first spotted in broad daylight by a group of golfers. They were a little shocked to see a man dancing naked on the course in the middle of their game. They called the police to approach the man, but as they approached, the figure disappeared. The incident was forgotten, until the same thing happened again. And again. The nude ghost appears to be Native American. He opens his mouth as if chanting, but no one hears his voice. Occasionally, his vibrant, circular dance occurs just inches above the ground. He has also been described as being quite gaunt—perhaps from performing the same tribal dance for 20 years?

FORT WORDEN
PORT TOWNSEND

You'd half expect to find ghosts at a former military base, especially among the bunkers and the cemetery. But beautiful Fort Worden has an unusual addition to the average ghostly occupants. Apparently, at the Guard House, an active soldier accidentally shot himself and died. He has haunted the building since the early 1900s, reluctant to give up his post or leave this earth. It is thought that he simply will not accept that the accident occurred and that he is truly dead. Port Townsend is rumored to be one of America's most haunted towns. At least the brave soldier is in good company.

THE "OTHER" SUICIDE BRIDGE
SEATTLE

Remember the "Suicide Bridge" mentioned earlier? What do you think happens to all those souls who spent their last agonizing moment jumping from the bridge? Some locals think they are doomed to retrace their steps. At least in one case, it appears to be so. On the less popular suicide bridge, I-5 in Seattle, in the late evening, a whispery ghost of a man in a black hat is seen walking back and forth across the bridge. Some say he has his dog with him, which is equally translucent.

BACK ROAD
CARNATION

Speaking of dogs...they apparently have spirits, too. An old campfire song by children's folk singer Ella Jenkins is called "Blue Walking." It tells the story of a dog looking for his master. The legend goes that one night in Carnation, local children were singing that song at camp. At the same time, a local ranger actually was searching for his lost dog. Nothing unusual about that, except that a woman driving along a back road near the camp reportedly saw a white, ghostly looking dog. Spooked, she accelerated the car, but moments later, three miles down the road, the same dog was watching and waiting. She couldn't figure out how the dog had moved so quickly...unless it was no longer subject to the physical rules of this plane.

GONZAGA UNIVERSITY
SPOKANE

Gonzaga University's Monaghan Hall in Spokane housed its own musical ghost from 1974 to 1975. The phantom of the music house made national headlines and is probably the most famous specter in Washington State history. Pianos in the mansion would start playing on their own—and these weren't player pianos. Sometimes faculty members heard an eerie flute melody, but whenever they went in search of the musician, there was no one to be seen. A cleaning woman on her night shift was startled to hear a simple melody being practiced on an organ long after closing hours. She went to the organ room, but the lights were off and the door was locked. When she unlocked the door, there was no one there. She even checked the windows, and they were locked. Soon after, a music instructor sat at the piano absentmindedly picking out a strangely familiar tune. The cleaning woman rushed to the door—she recognized the melody from the ghostly organ. The instructor then sat up abruptly. He'd recognized the tune from the flute. This musical guest was at least consistent.

Finally, Jesuit priest Father Walter Leedale was called in to recite prayers of exorcism throughout the building, floor by floor. And why not? Gonzaga is, after all, a Jesuit University. Father Leedale said that as he prayed, the crucifix around his neck began to swing from side to side. He smelled the strong odor of sulfur. He kept up, reciting the prayers for four days. The ritual appears to have kept the ghost away…for now.

MASONIC TEMPLE
TACOMA

Although the first Grand Lodge of Freemasonry was erected sometime around 1717, an absence of documentation leaves the actual origins of this fraternal organization a bit up in the air. They might not have been up and running exactly at the time of the Biblical King Solomon, but the king's palace—along with the castles of medieval England, the shrines of Islam and other examples of unique masonry—was certainly influential in determining the architecture these Freemasons chose for what eventually became their permanent, neighborhood meeting places. And so it is that while most of us might not know a wit about what's involved in being a Freemason, we all know a Masonic Temple when we see one. Washington has several examples of

Freemasonry architecture, and perhaps one of the best known among these is Tacoma's Masonic Temple. Built in 1926 or 1927, depending on the official source chosen, the Masonic portion of the building was built in the Greek Revival style, with Egyptian detailing inside, and was home to the Grand Lodge of the Free and Accepted Masons of Washington State. The adjoining theater, which was built about the same time, seats about 1620 people and includes a live stage, projection booth and movie screen. Although the theater is mostly used for live performances these days, which despite the grand appearance of the entire building actually includes wrestling bouts, it still has many of its original features, including a Kimball organ.

The building has gone through numerous changes, most notably with its name. In 1992 it was called the Saint Helens Convention Center, and then, three years later, it was renamed the Landmark Convention Center, at which time it was listed on the Federal Register of Historic Places. Touting itself as "one of the fastest growing convention facilities in the Northwest," the Landmark offers everything from the best in meeting rooms and catered banquets to a roof-top garden overlooking Commencement Bay.

But there are otherworldly goings-on that have etched the Landmark Convention Center and Temple Theatre into the minds of many—ghostly occurrences. As early as 1930, there were reports of ghosts appearing in various places in the theater. In one case, during a live stage show, a "he" ghost was thought to be watching a dancing girl. An incident in March 1972, in which a janitor was killed in an elevator accident, has added momentum to the belief that ghosts live in the building, especially because the now-repaired elevator appears to have a mind of its own, coming and going on it's own whim regardless of what efforts are put in to alter the problem. (By the way, in case you were interested, the elevator ghost is called Charlie.) And although some spirits just seem to linger around far longer than others do, they must be a fairly agreeable lot—folks don't seem to mind talking about them and business is, as they say, booming.

ABOUT THE AUTHORS

Bree Coven Brown

Bree is the co-author of *Shecky's NYC Apartment Guide* (Hangover Media, 2005) and has written for *Seattle Weekly, Seattle Magazine, New York* magazine and Msn.com among others. She was a regular columnist for *Curve* magazine for three years. Bree's work appears in more than 20 anthologies, including *Best of New York, New Millennium Writings, Generation Q,* the *City Dog* series, and *Erotic New York: A Guide to the Best Sex in the City.* Weird and wacky places she has lived include Hell's Kitchen, New York; Key West, Florida; Amsterdam, The Netherlands; and her most recent favorite, Seattle, Washington. Bree holds a degree in creative writing from Sarah Lawrence College. *Publishers Weekly* named her "one to watch."

Lisa Wojna

Lisa is the co-author of at least 12 trivia books, as well as being the sole author of nine other non-fiction books. She has worked in the community newspaper industry as a writer and journalist, her most memorable experience in that capacity being a trip to Ethiopia. Although writing and photography have been a central part of her life for as long as she can remember, it's the people behind every story that are her motivation and give her the most fulfillment.

ABOUT THE ILLUSTRATORS

Roger Garcia

Roger Garcia is a self-taught artist with some formal training who specializes in cartooning and illustration. He is an immigrant from El Salvador, and during the last few years, his work has been primarily cartoons and editorial illustrations in pen and ink. Recently he has started painting once more. Focusing on simplifying the human form, he uses a bright minimal palette and as few elements as possible. His work can be seen in newspapers, magazines, promo material and on www.rogergarcia.ca

Patrick Hénaff

Born in France, Patrick Hénaff is mostly self-taught. He is a versatile artist who has explored a variety of media under many different influences. He now uses primarily pen and ink to draw and then processes the images on computer. He is particularly interested in the narrative power of pictures and tries to use them as a way to tell stories.

Graham Johnson

Graham Johnson is an illustrator and graphic designer. When he isn't drawing or designing, he... well...he's always drawing or designing! On the off-chance you catch him not doing one of those things, he's probably cooking, playing tennis or poring over other illustrations.

Peter Tyler

Peter is a recent graduate of the Vancouver Film School's Visual Art and Design and Classical animation programs. Though his ultimate passion is in filmmaking, he is also intent on developing his draftsmanship and storytelling, with the aim of using those skills in future filmic misadventures.

More mad cap trivia from Blue Bike Books...

WASHINGTON TRIVIA: Weird, Wacky & Wild
Gina Spadoni & Lisa Wojna

Hundreds of factoids from every corner of the state! Learn about the first reported sighting of a UFO, the location of the world's single largest building, how a rookie crime reporter once worked side by side with a serial killer in Seattle and so much more!

Softcover • 5.25" X 8.25" • 224 pages • ISBN10 1-897278-18-7
• ISBN13 978-1-897278-18-5 • $14.95

CAT TRIVIA: Humorous, Heartwarming, Weird & Amazing
Diana MacLeod

Read more about the most popular pet in North America in this great collection of feline facts. How long have felines existed in North America? How high can a cat jump? What do you call a group of cats? Find the answers to these questions and many more.

Softcover • 5.25" X 8.25" • 224 pages • ISBN10 1-897278-26-8
• ISBN13 978-1-897278-26-0 • $14.95

DOG TRIVIA: Humorous, Heartwarming, Weird & Amazing
Wendy Pirk

Dogs—our best friends and hard-working companions. Humans have lived alongside them for millennia. But there's more to dogs than just tail wags and chasing tennis balls. In this fun collection of canine trivia, find out whether dogs really sweat using their tongues and why you're not the only one who talks to your dog while you're on vacation.

Softcover • 5.25" X 8.25" • 224 pages • ISBN10 1-897278-36-5
• ISBN13 978-1-897278-36-9 • $14.95

GROSS & DISGUSTING THINGS ABOUT THE HUMAN BODY
Joanna Emery

The human body may be a wonder of natural engineering but it also can be pretty gross and bad-smelling. In this fearless little book, find the answers to such profound questions as why are boogers green, why do farts smell, and where does belly button lint come from? Dare to read on!

Softcover • 5.25" X 8.25" • 232 pages • ISBN10 1-897278-25-X
• ISBN13 978-1-897278-25-3 • $14.95

Available from your local bookseller or by contacting the distributor, Lone Pine Publishing • 1-800-518-3541 • www.lonepinepublishing.com